Land of the Lakes

By the same author

FICTION

For Want of a Nail
The Second Inheritance
Without a City Wall
The Hired Man
A Place in England
The Nerve
Josh Lawton
The Silken Net
A Christmas Child
Autumn Manoeuvres
Kingdom Come

NON-FICTION

Speak for England

Land of the Lakes

MELVYN BRAGG

SECKER & WARBURG
LONDON

To Tom, three now, in the hope that he will
love the place as much as I do.

30596

914·273

First published in England 1983 by
Martin Secker & Warburg Limited
54 Poland Street, London W1V 3DF

Copyright © Melvyn Bragg 1983

British Library Cataloguing in Publication Data

Bragg, Melvyn
 Land of the lakes.
 1. Cumbria – History
 I. Title
 942.7'8   DA670.C93

ISBN 0–436–06715–3

Printed and bound in Great Britain by
Butler & Tanner Limited, Frome & London

Contents

Introduction   1
 1 The Beginnings   5
 2 Man versus Nature   21
 3 The History   31
 4 Language   62
 5 Work and Society   75
 6 Sports   105
 7 Legends and Traditions   118
 8 Opening up   133
 9 The Painters   178
10 The Writers   197
Epilogue   233
Acknowledgements   239
Index   241

Introduction

There is nowhere else like it in the world. Mountains as ancient as almost any on the planet, a history in stone and sculpture which can be seen today in monuments as spectacular and particular as you can imagine and a people whose roots and struggles have civilized a wilderness yet kept its nature magically intact. Many of my novels have been set in the Lake District; the time came when I wanted to find out more about it, to discover the reality which had underpinned the fiction. This book, then, is an exploration of that most elusive of worlds: one which we think we know so well that we take it for granted.

Like hundreds of thousands of others, I have walked and climbed here, biked and pushed my way up the passes to freewheel down the other side feeling as fast as a silent jet winging to earth from the clouds; I've rowed on the lakes and swum in them, been charged by a horned ram which might have come out of the Book of Revelations but was only trying to get back to its ewes in a field from which I had accidentally shepherded it away; and been lost in the heart of many a hundred mists. There are favourite villages, hidden spots, dangerous edges. When I was a child here I spoke the local dialect and still now feel moved at local markets when that Nordic knocking of warm consonants clinches the deals.

I lived here for my first twenty years; for the last ten I have returned five or six times a year; and the intervening decade only served to make me realize, when I came back, how truly extraordinary the Lake District is. This is confirmed whenever I meet anyone who has been here for a few weeks or even a few days; always there is the feeling that a unique place has been penetrated, that somehow they have been let in on a secret; the secret can be silence, beauty, friendliness, majesty, peace, harmony or all of these ... but they remember it ...

The secret is compounded of a vast variety of elements all concentrated in

1

a comparatively small arena. It is true that you could trot through the district in a day and a night: it is also true that you could live here a lifetime and still be taken to a ghyll or fell foreign to your experience. There is something awesome about the age and convolutions of the hills; and something even cosy about the circumscribed human scale of the place. It is a commonplace that the view can change dramatically every few feet; it is a commonplace that a walk could bring you to an Iron Age fortress, a Roman fort, a Nordic cross, a medieval church, and always with the accompaniment of that great stone signature which scrolls across the fells – the dry-stone walling; and it is a commonplace that you can walk the same paths as Wordsworth, Sir Walter Scott, Beatrix Potter, Coleridge, Keats, Dickens and many a thousand man and woman who have happily been lured here. Put all those commonplaces together and mix them with the violent unpredictability of the weather and you can begin to sense the intensity of life – a life which includes the mind-bending spans of years in the rocks as much as a rapid shift of light that can deliver a sky which Turner would have longed to paint.

It was not until I began to read for this book that I fully realized how much I had taken on. To attempt in a single volume to tackle geology, history, legends, language, painting, poetry, sports, towns, tourists, rock-climbers and industries as well as giving at least an impression of the place as it is today meant a mass of reading, looting and picking others' brains. Consequently my debts are vast. From the work of W. G. Collingwood to the books and practical help of William Rollinson, I have taken what I needed and the best return I can give is to aim for a book somewhere near the high traditions of scholarship set for the area.

Nobody should be fooled, however; nor, I am sure, will they be. I wanted to know about geology, for instance, because the formation of the land itself, that 500-million-year history we tread underfoot every day, struck me as the most romantic and essential part of this whole exploration. But, without any training in the subject, my only recourse was to read, learn and then pass on my results to an expert to check: waiting for his report was like being back at university contemplating an examination result. That section, then, is written from the outside: I can only speak of rooting about in Roughton Gill in an amateur fashion, nor can I pretend to have sought out unexpected outcrops in curious regions. Where being seen to be personally involved might help – I will do it: and at other times I'll stick to the facts.

Over the past few weeks I have looked down on the idyllic peacefulness of

Grasmere and Rydal Water and understood something of the passionate tranquillity of Dorothy Wordsworth on those same walks; talked with my neighbours about the hill farming which still holds firm; discovered a new small waterfall within an hour of the house I've lived in for ten years; seen sunsets over the Solway which have drawn me to the end of the day like a Japanese contemplative; been to a local game fair and to pubs where the sense of solidity rung as true as a golden guinea apparently resisting all the alloys of the restless changes characterizing so much of life elsewhere: in short, benefited, in those few ways and others, from the richness of a place which is still mysterious to me after years of living here and years of reading about it.

What is the final attraction of trying to put between two hard covers such varied information about one area? Perhaps it is the very limitation of the subject which allow us to get near a depth of understanding. We are such late arrivals on the planet. In so many ways so fragile, in others so powerful. To be able to see, in as little as a few days, both the gigantic play of world history and the more intimate marks of the human imprint and to be able to see it on such a scale is, again to use the word, magical. There are those who scoff at the sensations which some of us feel when we are in nature – and it is true that they are often so overwhelming that, as when faced by a calamity in our own lives, the best we can manage by way of description turn out to be clichés or truisms. But clichés have generally come about because they carry authentic responses; and truisms most often contain truth. To know one place as wholly as you can is to feel part of the scarcely comprehensible enormity of history. I am sure that there are those in Cornwall, in Yorkshire, in North Wales, in the Highlands and elsewhere who feel as strongly about their districts as I feel about this. Yet, speaking as you find, the district, the place itself, the imagination which has been bred from it and repaid it with great art, the armies and races which have moved across it and lodged reminders and descendants in it and the people who live here now combine to make the Lake District, for me, like nowhere else in the world.

Cumbria from 570 miles above the earth. This satellite photograph was taken on 28th May 1977.

1

The Beginnings

For some time I had known that the bedrock of the place was one of the oldest foundations on the planet: that knowledge of antiquity was like a romantic sub-text which enhanced an already well-fed sense of pleasure while walking on the fells. Only when I began to discover more, however, did the extent of the natural masterpiece claim its real due. The story is like an amazing melodrama, rolling slowly over epochs.

For almost 500 million years, through earthquake, ice, volcano, desert, flood and fire, the 900 square miles of the Lake District have heaved and moulded themselves into a geological phenomenon. Nowhere else in the world, in such a small area, is there so much diversity of rock, hill, shape and scene: from the parkland and meadows of the south, the seductive cleavages of forest in the bosom of gentle slopes: to the bared volcanic rocks of the heartland with sheer falls, sudden ascents, corries, deep, glaciated valleys, crags and dangers: on to the Northern Fells where a gentle herd of gigantic and ancient elephants seem to have lain down to sleep, their wrinkled hides lightly blanketed with bracken; to the Lakes themselves, late-comers like the tourists who come to look on them. Lakes, meres, tarns, waters and waterfalls, each, again, as different as one human face from another, reflecting, separating and enhancing the fells like so many handmaidens at the feet of so many thrones. Forests too, new and old, and the clear remains of human settlements from more than 7,000 years ago. From Bronze Age circles to nuclear power stations, what has been fashioned in its foundations by nature has been modelled and re-surfaced by man. The fame which the Lake District enjoys comes from that, perhaps most of all: the clash between elemental pressures and human forces. Out of it has come a place, as

Jonathan Otley, the father of
Lakeland geology.

John Ruskin said, 'of precious chasing and embossed work'.

The whole district is lapped by plains to the north, sands to the south, the sea to the west and bare uplands to the east, so that it is not unlike an island; and that perhaps is why those who come here so often say they feel 'cut off'. And like an island, it has attracted legends, myths and invaders.

For me, for years, the fells themselves stood some distance off, ever present, never known, as much of a dream as a real place. I was born and brought up about ten miles from the northern entrances to the Lake District and throughout my early childhood the mountains were there – Skiddaw outstanding – distant, to be glanced at every day but no more than that. In those days of the Second World War and timidity in travel, our occasional treats were to bowl down to the sea. Maybe the hills looked too difficult. But, like others, like most of those who visit the fells today, I found they had some sort of existence in my imagination. They were like the promise of a good story, and the hint of an adventurous world. Now that I know it more, the adventure has, if anything, grown even more seductive.

For still today what I get most from it is what I drew from it when I was a boy: an atmosphere. Especially just before nightfall – the time when the place most comes alive in my mind. Then the feeling of a dream or a mirage is peaceful and powerful. As the darkness settles on the fells, deeper shades of blue and grey and purple co-mingle to such a sensuous thickness that you want to thrust your bare arm into it and daub yourself with this ancient power. It is the potency and the antiquity, both, which draw you in.

The history of the landscape is the subject of this chapter. I want to tell it as a time-walk. For it is possible, in this compact space, to travel through 500 million years. The journeys undertaken by men in space seem almost trivial by comparison. Here, in the matter of a few days, you can walk through half a billion years of time. I have worked out and visited the best places to go to in order to get a sense of this unrolling from the beginning of the world to the arrival of men and my new knowledge of the time-scale involved has made it enjoyably daunting.

Start on Skiddaw in the north. Stand on the hefty slopes of Skiddaw, and a few inches beneath your feet are some of the oldest formations of rock in the world. Best of all, be there at dusk.

About 570 million years ago, a new era began in British geological history. The seas were full of life: many animals with hard shells appeared: and for about 150 million years those seas deposited thick muddy sediment over most of Britain.

This is why it is best to go to Skiddaw as it is growing darker. Then, ankle deep in bracken, you can better imagine the state of the earth at that time. No hills, no valleys, no land. A shallow sea would have covered everything. The deposits of mud later to be changed into slates by earth movements and pressures were building the very foundations of the place. Almost ten thousand feet of solid Cumberland was to come out of this sediment. And later, when the last ice age gave the hills most of their present shape, not only Skiddaw but Saddleback, Mellbreak, the Grasmoor group and, in the south-west, Black Combe were all to be embodied with darkish slates. There are slight distinctions – so that you get the Kirkstile slates, and the Mosser slates named after localities around Loweswater. But there is a large degree of uniformity and these dark twilight slates remain for me the true tone of the district. Houses, barns and walls seem to grow out of the ground in this slate. As the slates grew out of the shallow sea. This is where the adventure began. A slow, late, lonely walk back down alongside Dash Beck can evoke all the vast nervous fears of that begin-ning: Genesis, underfoot.

The high undulating smooth-surfaced shape characteristic of Skiddaw and the other slate mountains suddenly changes, about twelve miles south, into the

Crinkle Crags from Pike of Blisco. The name is derived not from the profile but from the Old Norse *kringla*, a circle – the crags which encircle the head of Great Langdale.

jagged irregular outlines of the Borrowdale volcanic rocks. Within a few yards, two epochs crunch together. This volcanic region drew gasps of horror, real and feigned, from the eighteenth- and early nineteenth-century visitors to the Lakes. 'Horrid', 'barren', 'rude', 'awesome', 'truly dreadful' – the adjectives were heaped on this rugged and forbidding central area by Gray, West and many others. Just as the majestic rump of Skiddaw characterizes the slate mountains, so perhaps Crinkle Crags, which look as they sound, characterize this volcanic region. And they bring us about 50 million years nearer the present.

About 450 million years ago there were fiercely active volcanoes in the heartland of the place. Stand, nowadays, up in Rosthwaite, on the Langdales or anywhere in that region, and imagine that for the length of about one million

The end product of volcanic activity and ice action – the rugged profile of the Langdale Pikes

years, in Ordovician times, well after the Skiddaw Slates had been laid down, volcanoes of the fury of Etna and Vesuvius spouted lava and fine ash thousands of feet into the air. The fine ash fell into shallow water and subsequently became the green slates of Honister, Elterwater and Coniston. And, oddly, just as the northern Skiddaw range has an isolated cousin in the south – Black Combe – so these Borrowdale Volcanics pop up to the north of Skiddaw in summits such as High Pike. It's a pleasing symmetry.

The rocks in this region are a geologist's trove. Different names have been given to the varied rocks, such as the Harter Fell Andesites, the Langdale Rhyolites and the Sty Head Garnetiferous series. And because the lava and ashes present 'a varied resistance to denudation' (Monkhouse) the silhouettes in the region are remarkably hard edged, angular and spectacular.

9

Gimmer Crag, Great Langdale. Most of the famous rock climbs lie within the Borrowdale Volcanic group of rocks.

One of the 'classic' climbs, Kern Knotts Crack on Great Gable. Half the genius of these early climbers was to identify a challenge; the other half was to rise to it.

Where geologists dream, rock-climbers conquer, and if you trace out a map of all the major rock climbs in the Lake District and lay it over the Ordnance Survey – all the great climbs are inside this region of Borrowdale Volcanics.

Still going south, we cross a narrow band of Coniston Limestone which cuts across the land like grey string around the bulging parcel of hills. This is usually dated in the Ordovician era. It is interesting to walk or drive along it – the road from Ambleside to Coniston is as good a spot as any: to the north you see the crags which came from lava spat out 450 million years ago; in the south there are the low gentle slopes of the Silurian age, laid down 400 million years ago.

The southern block is the last great layer of Cumbria which, in this respect, like Gaul, was divided into three parts. The shales, slates, grits and flags of the

Silurian age are probably best seen around Hawkshead and Grizedale Forest. It's a well-wooded part now. When it was formed, it too grew in the marine sediments of a shallow sea and the final shapes now reflect those of the Northern Fells – undulating and round backed, except that they are not as high and they are more evenly undulating.

In those 100 million years, then, the three great slabs of the place were laid down. These three zones, so clearly defined then and now, come out of such an age and time of movement on the globe that it is as awesome as the ever receding boundaries of an ever expanding universe. You can visit them all in a day and enjoy stretching imagination to picture the process whose present continuing story is at your feet.

The next 50 million years could be called the time of the Intrusions and by the time we reach 350 million years ago, granite and other complex crystalline rocks are present. Molten rock had solidified slowly. The granite is all over the place: to the west in Eskdale, to the north in Carrock Fell, to the east around Shap. It is difficult though – and professional geologists have said as much – to describe the differences between the present look of these granite intrusions and the volcanic series. Some intrusions – crystalline rocks – are still there for the taking: for anyone interested in rocks, large areas are still a delight for scavengers and connoisseurs. Howk Ghyll near Caldbeck can be highly recommended; even an amateur like me returns home with a sackful of rocks ruining the flimsy picnic-haversack.

The next appearance of note, along this time-walk, is that of Carboniferous Limestone which lies like a broken ring around the rim of the three main blocks. You can see it in the south at Grange-over-Sands; in the north at the Howk in Caldbeck; to the west at Frizington; to the east near Penrith. There's a gap along the west coast between Maryport and Whitehaven where coal was found. For at this time too, the Coal Measures were laid down, and many of them lie now as they lay then – under the sea. The sea of Cumbria, though (strange thought in the present northern climate), was, at that time, as tropical and swampy as something at the mouth of the Amazon. Wandering on the thin turf which covers the limestone it is worth remembering the steamy entanglements of vegetation and earth which hissed and sucked the surface plantation down into the ground. And through that ground trickled the water which entered the limestone; the vegetation became the coal and iron ore, the rich red haematite which once threatened the coastal plain with prosperity.

After the tropics, the desert. There was a time – a long time – when Cumbria

11

looked like the Sahara. This was about 250 million years ago and it left us what is called the New Red Sandstone. You can see it at the northern edge of the Lakes, in the east around Penrith, in the south in Furness where that lovely abbey is built of it – but the most dramatic place to see the sandstone is on the cliffs of St Bees. There you can stand and attempt to grapple with the fact that inland, as far as you can see, there was a barren, parched, empty, sun-battered desert.

Seas, volcanoes, tropics and deserts bring us about half-way on our journey. Cumbria has been swept up by climates and forces quite foreign to it now. At the end of those 250 million years, the foundations are laid, the rocks are in place, the pressing and grinding was going on as it goes on still. The climate will keep changing, the place will look very different over this quiescent 200 million years – the limestone for example is being steadily eroded – but the substructure is deposited on the planet. In the next stage it is formed and given its present contours.

2

About 350 million years ago there were the first significant earth-movements – called the Caledonian – in which the rocks laid down so far were buckled into a ridge which ran east-north-east to west-south-west through Skiddaw. For the next 50 million years, erosion ground the rocks down until 'the broad pattern of the surface rocks of today had been revealed' (Monkhouse). Then there were deposits of fresh matter.

Over 100 million years later there was another mountain-building epoch – called the Hercynian – which shoved up the limestone strata in the middle of the area. This again was followed by erosion and again new deposits – this time of New Red Sandstone. Which brings us to our greatest time leap – from 250 million to 15 million years ago.

If you had looked around then you would have seen nothing to foreshadow the present Lake District: no coastline, no lakes, no discernible fells, no vegetation – it was a desert landscape. What happened 15 million years ago was a final earth-movement which gave the place its present layout. This process – called 'doming up' – is most easily described like this: think of a tablecloth; put your hands down at either side of it; push in slowly towards the centre. The resultant ridges and wrinkles are the 'doming up' process. This is what happened in the centre of the Lakes around Great Gable and Scafell about 15 million years ago, and it was that which gave the Lake District its distinctive

The volcanic fells of upper Eskdale.

shape. It established the radial drainage pattern first noted down by Wordsworth in his *Guide to the Lakes*. His description remains the classic introduction
to the lie of the land. He asks his reader:

> . . . to place himself with me, in imagination, upon some given point; let it be the
> top of either of the mountains, Great Gavel [Gable] or Scafell; or, rather, let us
> suppose our station to be a cloud hanging midway between those two mountains, at
> not more than half a mile's distance from the summit of each, and not many yards
> above their highest elevation; we shall then see stretched at our feet a number of
> valleys, not fewer than eight, diverging from the point, on which we are supposed to
> stand, like spokes from the nave of a wheel. First, we note, lying to the South-East,
> the vale of Langdale*, which will conduct the eye to the long lake of Winandermere,

* Anciently spelt Langden, and so called by the old inhabitants to this day – *dean*, from which the
latter part of the word is derived, being in many parts of England a name for a valley.

stretched nearly to the sea; or rather to the sands of the vast bay of Morcamb, serving here for the rim of this imaginary wheel; – let us trace it in a direction from the South-East towards the South, and we shall next fix our eyes upon the vale of Coniston, running up likewise from the sea, but not (as all the other valleys do) to the nave of the wheel, and therefore it may be not inaptly represented as a broken spoke sticking in the rim. Looking forth again, with an inclination towards the West, we see immediately at our feet the vale of Duddon, in which is no lake, but a copious stream winding among fields, rocks, and mountains, and terminating its course in the sands of Duddon. The fourth vale, next to the observed, viz that of the Esk, is of the same general character as the last, yet beautifully discriminated from it by peculiar features. Its stream passes under the woody steep upon which stands Muncaster Castle, the ancient seat of the Penningtons, and after forming a short and narrow estuary enters the sea below the small town of Ravenglass. Next, almost due west, look down into, and along the deep valley of Wastdale, with its little chapel and half a dozen neat dwellings scattered upon a plain of meadow and corn-ground intersected with stone walls apparently innumerable, like a large piece of lawless patch-work, or an array of mathematical figures, such as in the ancient schools of geometry might have been sportively and fantastically traced out upon sand. Beyond this little fertile plain lies, within a bed of steep mountains, the long, narrow, stern, and desolate lake of Wastdale; and, beyond this, a dusky tract of level ground conducts the eye to the Irish Sea. The stream that issues from Wastwater is named the Irt, and falls into the estuary of the river Esk. Next comes in view Ennerdale, with its lake of bold and somewhat savage shores. Its stream, the Ehen or Enna, flowing through a soft and fertile country, passes the town of Egremont, and the ruins of the castle – then, seeming, like the other rivers, to break through the barrier of sand thrown up by the winds on this tempestuous coast, enters the Irish Sea. The vale of Buttermere, with the lake and village of that name, and Crummock-water, beyond, next present themselves. We will follow the main stream, the Coker, through the fertile and beautiful vale of Lorton, till it is lost in the Derwent, below the noble ruins of Cockermouth Castle. Lastly, Borrowdale, of which the vale of Keswick is only a continuation, stretching due north, brings us to a point nearly opposite to the vale of Winandermere with which we began. From this it will appear that the image of a wheel, thus far exact, is little more than one half complete; but the deficiency on the eastern side may be supplied by the vale of Wytheburn, Ullswater, Haweswater, and the vale of Grasmere and Rydal; none of these, however, run up to the central point between Great Gavel and Scawfell. From this, hitherto our central point, take a flight of not more than four or five miles eastward to the ridge of Helvellyn, and you will look down upon Wytheburn and St John's Vale, which are a branch of the vale of Keswick; upon Ullswater, stretching due east: – and not far beyond to the south-east (though from this point not visible) lie the vale and lake of

Scafell Crag and Pulpit Rock. The popular footpath, Lord's Rake, follows the base of the crag and ascends the gully on the right.

Haweswater; and lastly, the vale of Grasmere, Rydal, and Ambleside, brings you back to Winandermere, thus completing, though on the eastern side in a somewhat irregular manner, the representative figure of the wheel.

The only thing to add is – go up Gable and Scafell and see for yourselves the clear effects of something that happened in a place essentially formed almost 15 million years before the first man appeared.

With another leap we come to one million years ago when two dramatic events occurred: it is at that time that man-like apes began to evolve into ape-like man: and the ice ages got under way. For the first, there is no evidence in Cumbria; for the second, the ice ages, there is evidence on every fellside. There were to be four ice ages and they were to dig and chisel out the contours, the enfoldments and the intricacies of the place.

3

'The most powerful agent in the history of the landscape has been the sculpture of the rocks by the plucking and grinding of ice during the successive glaciations of the last million years' (W. H. Pearsall and Winifred Pennington). A million years ago, the place looked like Greenland – great ice sheets stretched to the horizon and the tiny rock tips of mountains peeped through like molehills through snow. Very occasionally nowadays, you can be on top of a fell after there have been heavy snowfalls and then you can have some literal appreciation of what it must have been like a million years ago.

The ice brought about major changes. The movement of the glaciers down the valleys – an extraordinary and terrifying sight that must have been, although there is no evidence that there was anyone there to see it – gouged and smoothed as it went. Most of the overlapping spurs were eroded; the deep V-shaped valleys with steep sides were modified; the fact that some valleys held less ice than others meant that some were more deeply rutted than others, which resulted in valleys being left to hang above each other as at Sour Milk Gill, near Grasmere; tarns were isolated high in the hills as a result of the overdeepening by and then the melting of the glaciers; corries and arêtes such as that at Striding Edge and Swirrel Edge are clear evidence of the fierce grinding down to the bone of the rock that the glaciers carved as the ice-snout crept down and then melted back in four successive invasions.

The ice was a great carrier and dumper. Huge tonnages of Shap granite, for

Striding Edge and Red Tarn, both the product of glacial erosion.

example, were dislodged, broken off and taken for a hundred miles, and all around the Lakes sand and clay were scraped off and swept away to be deposited in places where they changed the landscape. All around the lowland area – the Kendal district provides the best example – there are drumlins – small boulder clay mounds, more hummocks than hills – reminders of the time the ice crunched through Cumbria and carved it into the final shape we see today.

When the glaciers retreated, about 10,000 years ago (although they did have a small comeback later), they left the relief map of the present land; no vegetation whatsoever; and the lakes. Once there were almost certainly more lakes than there are now – there could well have been a lake in Great Langdale and a large tarn on the top of Carrock for example. Yet despite the lakes giving their name to the district and its distinctive character to the area, they may be just a temporary, passing feature. Already many of them are markedly smaller than they were even a few hundred years ago. Professional geologists tend to be a little patronizing about the lakes because of their comparative youth.

The lakes had arrived, but in a bleak and barren spot. The ice had scraped everything away and for a time the only movement on the land was in the screes which cracked and slid as the ice deep in the recesses of rock expanded and cracked open the surfaces. This erosion still goes on, with the Wast Water screes as its most dramatic testament. At Wast Water in winter you can not only see clear evidence of the effect of the ice age, you can very easily believe you are still living in it.

The ice put the gloss on a story which had moved through gigantic spans of time. Deposits of slate-mud; volcanic eruptions; earth movements; denudation followed by more deposits – all this had now been sculpted by ice. From now on the story is of drapery, as it were, of the covering, the surface and look of things. And increasingly the landscape reflects the men who lived in it.

4

But first – between ten and eight thousand years ago – the new vegetation crept in – rather like that which can be seen in northern Norway today; reindeer moss and lichen which you can still find on peaks such as Great Gable. Over those two or three thousand years, the empty, ice-shocked valleys seeded alder; up the sides of the valleys, oak, ash and elm grew; above that, Scots pine and yet further up, willow and dwarf birch until the whole district became one vast dense woodland. And it was just at that time that man appeared.

The Langdale Pikes from The Band. The central scree descending from Pike of Stickle marks the approximate site of the stone axe factory.

Cumbrian man appears to have taken his time to get here. In the Thames Valley, for example, there is evidence of Old Stone Age man from 18,000 years ago. Cumbria at that time was on the edge of one of the great ice caps – no place for settlement, and not even, later, for Middle Stone Age man despite the gallant remains of a few tiny flints. It is Neolithic, New Stone Age, man, who makes his home and his impact here. The challenge was the forest. It had to be cleared for animals and for crops. The response of Neolithic man was the Langdale stone axe.

To continue the time-walk through this man-made period, the best place to begin is at Pike of Stickle, 2,300 feet above sea-level. Seven to eight thousand years ago, this was just at the edge of the great entanglement of the Lakeland forests – now disappeared but for haunting small woods. At Pike of Stickle, on the scree, an axe factory was discovered.

These axes were made from porcellenite, a finely grained volcanic ash which chips exactly as flint does. It has a very sharp cutting edge and even today, you can cut your finger by trailing it along the edge. The axes were shaped there but they were finished down on the coast where the sandstone on the beaches and the fine quartz sand provided the means for polishing. There is a perfect example of a hafted axe (the only one found in Britain) in the British Museum. It is hafted in a wooden haft and was found at Beckermet near the west Cumbrian coast.

From now on, the landscape is changed more by man than by nature. That Langdales axe-man was the first of many destroyers and creators who have hacked and modelled the surface patterns we now see. But just a few feet below that surface, those hundreds of millions of years live on and anyone with senses to feel can get intimations of the apparent immortality of slate, granite, rock and shale, still shifting, still changing, bound on a course whose beginnings we can glimpse in samples but scarcely imagine and whose future will undoubtedly outlive us all. It is that present and immediate apprehension of a scale so very much bigger than ourselves and so obscure in its origins and in its ends which gives to every walk and climb the resonance and excitement of limitless time.

2

Man
versus
Nature

Charcoal burning often
involved the care of
several pitsteads at
various stages of 'burn';
consequently many
'colliers' lived for weeks
on end in turf-built huts
in the woodlands.

What have we done with this majestic inheritance of land and lakes, forests, rivers and falls?

The most striking impact was made by the man with the axe. He began the cropping of Cumbria, up on the Langdale heights. Iron Age man took up the axe and moved into the valleys then enmeshed in ancient forests and the domain of game and predators. The Romans cleared the way for roads and forts; the Anglian farmers felled the lowlands; the Norsemen sailed up the rivers and took their axes up to the higher ground. But still in the Middle Ages, the Lake District boasted forests as dense and more extensive than any in Britain. Industry levelled most of that: charcoal burners singed the land bare around their settlements; the sheep farming industry of the Cistercians encouraged further clearances and, towards the end of the sixteenth century, the most massive axe blows of all were delivered by the German miners who came to Keswick to exploit the mineral wealth of the district and were so greedy for fuel that they ran out of trees and opened a coalmine on the coast. The trees that were left slowly toppled down over the next three hundred years for war and industry until now the overwhelming surface of the place is bare.

I like it so. Forests have their power and in the stub ends that remain up here the sense of vernal complexity and that never-quite-silent life makes you want to

Charcoal burners and huts, Kirkby, south Cumbria, c. 1905.

stand and listen to this other world going about its work. Childhood visions of Sherwood Forest or later encounters with forests in the books of Charles Read or the paintings of Ucello, push into mind the romantic congestion of those settlements of trees and shrubs and the place becomes an endless image of paths and glades. Even a tiny stump of oak near my house can induce that feeling of another world which is to be entered with care but returns unexpected pleasures at every other turn.

Yet the bold bareness of the fells has so many advantages. To be able to see so much of the shape of the other hills when you are coming down Skiddaw towards Keswick, for example, is never dull. The few plots of trees which still hug some hillsides are nowhere near as compelling as those bare pelts, bank after bank receding south to the Scafell axis, where the light darts over the bracken and a glint of the sun brings out all shades from the rock outcrops.

There are the expansive views, then, which is one bonus of bareness. Another is the continuous awareness that you are near the bone of the place. Little interferes with the line of the hills, the gullies and ghylls, the creeks and dips of land. You can mesmerize yourself – as I sometimes do just leaning over the gates and looking over on to the Caldbeck fells – by staring and feeling that it has always been like that. It is not unlike looking at the sea – the same sense of awe, of something now docile, now treacherous, immense always and, however well known, ultimately unknowable. It is this oceanic feeling, I think, which draws the real aficionados of Lakeland up on to High Street or teases them to seek out the fells at their most out-of-season times: the bareness enhances the feeling of great solitude. Again, you need not go far for it. I remember going up Blen-

Pillar mountain and Ennerdale forestry; the insistent lines of these unexciting trees have given rise to considerable criticism.

Wasdale Head from Westmorland Cairn, Great Gable. The earlier network of irregular fields on the valley floor contrasts with the later and more regular enclosures on the fellside.

cathra one day, from the north, a bright day in the middle of winter, and never meeting a soul from start to finish. By the end of the walk I was willing everyone to keep away. The isolation was marvellous. It had been like scudding across empty waters.

And there is often the best of both worlds because the trees have not entirely gone. The fringes of many of the lakes have their trees; and looking down on Grasmere from up towards Grisedale you are aware of trees plentiful enough to charm that lake into its character; Wordsworth had the lushness he wanted there.

He detested the attempt to cover the bare uplands with larch plantations – re-afforestation began systematically in the eighteenth century. I disagree with many of his prejudices – from his objections to whitewashed cottages to his disgust about the railway – but here I go along with him. I appreciate the need for wood: I understand that re-afforestation holds together surfaces which would otherwise slither away altogether; I can even listen to those who like what

An ancient craft – the building of a dry-stone wall.

has been done and once or twice around Ennerdale I have felt that it was not too bad. But they fit too neatly, these drilled rows of firs: in a place where the naturalness is so dominating the man-made incursion of these unexciting trees subtracts from the landscape.

Yet not all additions are diminishing. The dry-stone walls, the thousands, even tens of thousands, of miles which segment the area, seem to me to be the very finest contribution to the landscape. They were built mainly in the eighteenth and nineteenth centuries as the enclosure system replaced the open field system and they were built by the same sort of men who built the Pyramids, the Parthenon, Chartres, the railways and the motorways: labourers whose names are forgotten. They would work high up on the fells in all weathers, quarrying the stone around them as they piled it into the infinite shapes necessary for a wall which would endure the worst storms and last for centuries. Because they are built from the rocks they stand on, they melt snugly into the hills. The fact that they divide the fells into irregular shapes humanizes the scale of the heights; while the knowledge of those gangs of men piling stone

25

The double span of the bridge at Grange-in-Borrowdale.

on stone for miserable wages, sleeping out in all weathers, gradually leaving a trail behind them as clear as a snail's track and as slow to fabricate, is always moving.

The bridges too are an embellishment: they stand to the grandeur of the walls rather as the waterfalls stand to the lakes. Who can resist leaning over Stockley Bridge looking at that deep pool of mountain water and deciding to have a quick dip on the way back from Gable? (How few, though, carry that out!) There's the ancient Monk's Bridge and other packhorse bridges such as Throstle Garth or Wasdale Head; the serene double span across Grange, over-popular Ashness – all of them providing lingering points on a walk. The apparent simplicity of the building brings, again, a comfortable note to the full orchestration of the fells. And once again, for anyone with the inclination to dream, the knowledge that each bridge has seen ten thousand journeys, on foot, on mule, on horse, by carriage, bike and car, has taken armies across and visitors on their way, cattle to milking and Lakelanders to their homes – this certainly entertains – and excuses – me while I sit thankfully on the parapet and look around at the fells I have climbed or intend to climb.

A further way in which men have affected the landscape has been by gorging into it for minerals. There are scores of minerals to be found in the district

26

A splendid cruck-timbered barn at Field Head Farm near Hawkshead.

including garnet, jaspar, silver and malachite. The most common quarrying, though, has been for slate – you can see the large quarries on the side of Coniston Old Man – or granite – at Embleton and Shap – and haematite, lead and copper in the Keswick area. There are those who consider those to be scars on the landscape. I can see the point of that argument, but (especially since finding out something about geology) I enjoy them as specimen centres, open laboratories, in some cases open displays of the rocks we live on. While I am always conscious, even at a quarry as well worked as Embleton, that only the top surface has been scratched: somehow, all our energy still gets such a little way into the heart of the matter: which is comforting; so much remains.

The last two assaults on the landscape are the buildings and the tourists.

The great rebuilding in stone which took place in most places in the sixteenth century came to Cumbria rather late – between 1640 and 1750. There are one or two examples of building which retain their timber framework – such as Field Head at Hawkshead or Wall End in Great Langdale. But the great majority of farms and cottages were built in that century and now, two or three hundred years later, they settle as naturally on the fells and in the valleys as the cattle and sheep which so often cluster about them. There is no house so pleasant as the plain double-fronted Cumbrian farmhouse with its classical line, its comfortable solidity and its siting most generally protected from the worst wind but

Fell walkers on the summit of The Old Man of Coniston, Easter Sunday, 1982.

facing on to an enviable view. They are all around me in this district; and the fact that they are most often working places, backed by barns and byres, gives them an air of self-sufficiency which seems lacking in almost any other domestic building. The cottages too, such as the one I live in, built at the same time though on a smaller scale, share in those qualities – often driven into the hillside, sacrificing the view for protection against the weather.

Hamlets, villages and towns have settled over such a long time in this place that the feeling is of a welcome break in the roll of landscape rather than an alien dumping on it. Generally speaking, the stone is local and sometimes the effect can be quietly ravishing. Penrith, for example, is full of the warm sandstone found in the soil and abandoned quarries round about; Kendal is a limestone town; Keswick's colours come from the slate while a darker slate suffuses Ambleside. When you look down on these towns, they have a particular glow about them which points up the prevailing tone. The effect is curious: it is as if the landscape has gathered itself together for a show – of mellowness at Penrith, of slate-grey subtleties at Keswick, of chaste bluish austerity at Kendal. It's the stone itself which gives this concentrated effect, almost as if it were glad of an opportunity to show what it can do.

Thanks partly to the care of those who run the National Park and to a still fairly widespread habit of careful behaviour, the impact of the visitors to this

28

Twentieth-century changes: the roundabout on the A66 north of Keswick.

district is nowhere near as disastrous as in many other places. Indeed there is something enjoyable in being part of the struggle which plods towards Striding Edge or hugs the path around Scafell: while for those who disdain company, for about forty-eight weeks of the year the place is hardly touched and at any time of year anyone determined to be alone can soon find a solitary walk. Caravan and camping sites are carefully camouflaged; the traffic along the narrow valley roads can be intolerable – but few people want to stay in a car for very long when they come here. The car park at Hawkshead has robbed that lovely place of its charm; the congestion in Grasmere makes you feel the poor village ought to be sent away for a period of convalescence; the roundabout on the northern side of Keswick adds nothing to the beauty of the region; the orange anoraks which speckle the fells on summer days provide as inappropriate and garish a contrast to the local colours as you could possibly imagine – but generally the visitors, like the locals, see the landscape as something to be cherished.

The National Park rangers make and mend throughout the year and this civilized wilderness is now in their hands. The public on the whole responds to them. The landscape has undoubtedly won in its fight with men: almost without throwing a punch, you might say, for after all the cropping and digging, the building and tourism, wherever you look you see the fells apparently empty and completely undisturbed following their indifferent slow evolution.

The men who have come to the most satisfying terms with the land are the hill farmers. The hamlet I live in has three farms and five other dwellings. It is the farmers who hold it together. To see them daily up on the fells with their sheep or cattle, hear them out in the middle of the night lambing in what is often a bitter spring, be with them in pubs and at market while they retail the experiences of the day – I have met many diffident hill farmers and some almost suffocatedly shy but none who, once started, can fail to tell stories of their day which wrap you into interest as tightly as they themselves have been involved in the action – to live among them is to see that there is indeed a struggle between men and the landscape which can have a rich outcome for both parties. These men know about their fells and fields and look after them; they live off them but do not plunder them; they use the landscape but return interest to it. Above all they know that it is there, all about them, there before and after their day, to be respected, admired, discussed, worried over and cared for. As long as these farmers hold to the centre of the fells, then that delicate balance between nature and men will be harmonious. If they go, not all the National Parks in the world can save the place from becoming a mere playground.

A nineteenth-century Lakeland shepherd.

3

The History

1

The history of the Lake District from the Bronze Age is largely the story of a natural fortress continuously evading conquest because it contained little the invaders wished to hold or loot. By contrast, the history of the borderlands to the north of the district is written in strife and passages of arms. The higher ground often became a refuge and in some ways a centre of independence. If Grasmere, near the centre of the Lakes, meant very little, ever, to anyone, in terms of war and conquest, Carlisle – the Border City – meant everything to Kings of Scotland, Strathclyde, France, Northumbria and England. It is a nice irony that one of the most battered castles in Britain, Carlisle, rests just a few miles north of the largest and most undisturbed natural fortification in the land.

2

There is evidence that there were settlements on the western coast about 7000 BC. At the Isle of Walney, Cartmel, St Bees and Drigg, small flints have been found which indicate that Mesolithic man secured a toe-hold on the coastline where at that time there would be little or no forest and plenty of fish. But although a presence is now certain, impact, from excavations so far, appears to have been minimal.

It is later, with the New Stone Age men, who arrived here about 5500 BC, that the Lake District enters into the story of humankind. William Rollinson has described their impact as 'arguably more dramatic and far reaching than either the Agricultural or the Industrial Revolutions of the 18th and 19th Century'.

A hafted polished
stone axe from
Ehenside Tarn
near Beckermet.

Their most substantial achievement was to attack the forest, by then deeply
entrenched right up to the mountain tops. To do this they made stone axes,
quarried and roughened at Pike of Stickle, Glaramara and Scafell, polished on
the coast and found subsequently in Southern England, Yorkshire, the Isle of
Man and elsewhere. When hafted – given handles – these axes became prize
agricultural tools to be used as a hoe or mattock. I have one on my desk as I
write; it still gives the thumb a tingle as you draw it across the polished edge.
This was the essential implement of thousands of years of history.

Land was cleared and sown with summer grain; stock was reared to supple-
ment the game and deer and fish. The people who lived here spun, wove and
made pots. A few of their caves have been traced in the limestone scars in
Warton Crag around Carnforth, for example. A tarn drained at Ehenside has
yielded substantive booty for the British Museum. There are burial mounds at
Raiset Pike near Sunbiggin Tarn, and henge monuments from Late Stone Age
Neolithic man (about 2000 BC) at Mayburgh, Eamont Bridge, where a huge ring
of cobbles, some fifteen feet high, with a single entrance to the east, encloses an
area of about one and a half acres. They discovered and used copper, lead and
iron; they also found silver for personal adornment.

The local inhabitants found by the Romans to be working in iron were the
direct descendants of the stone-axe makers, whose span in the Lake District has
been the longest and the most important of all. Whoever they were, these men
and women were the founders of what we call the Lake District. Their artisan

32

Man's response to the challenge of the forest: roughed-out and polished stone axes from Langdale Fell.

talents sustained them here for as long as the Pharaohs ruled Egypt and they made it a place fit to live in.

There is only little evidence of war. The land ran with game; fish and fuel were everywhere. It could be that it was the golden age – for certainly those people were intelligent. They could live where we would starve. And for almost four thousand years they had the place to themselves.

3

The Beaker People – so called because of the drinking cups found in their burial mounds – arrived here about 2000 BC at the end of their long push from the centre of Europe, possibly via Ireland. It was warmer and calmer then and the Irish Sea – possible to cross in small vessels – nurtured a culture, trading and fishing with South-West Scotland, North-West England, North Wales, the Isle of Man and of course Ireland itself, which again and again sent over civilizing and labouring forces to the east. A few hundred years later, again possibly from Ireland, bronze tools were introduced. Bronze Age relics were found on Askham Fell, for example, and there are small Bronze Age cairns in great numbers in the Ulverston area, between the Duddon and the Ehen and over in the upper Eden Valley in the east. Once again, there is nothing like a visit to ignite the imagination and set off a conversation about what they were *for*. More than sixty Bronze Age sites have now been excavated.

A romantic view of the Castlerigg Circle.

But the outstanding remains from this time – about 1500 BC – are the great stone circles. Castlerigg, Long Meg and her Daughters and Swinside are the three best examples. They have sat silent in the Lake District for about 3,500 years. They have the mysterious attractions of Stonehenge and have been subjected to as many interpretations.

The concentric circles and some of the motifs on the stones (these are best seen at Salkeld – Long Meg) point to a connection with the spectacular passage graves of the Bend of the Boyne in Ireland – yet nothing which has been discovered in the large stone circles of Lakeland suggests that they were graveyards. There are no fire-hearths, which suggests they were not used for sacrifice. They seem ill equipped and over elaborate to be cattle kraals. It has been suggested that they were part of the plan of the Egyptian priesthood to establish astronomical check-points over Western and North-Western Europe, but that beguiling notion has gone the way of the Druids – into fantasy rather than fact. There is no one agreed solution to the questions who built them and for what purpose.

I visited Castlerigg again the other week. It is extraordinarily beautiful, thirty-nine irregular boulders placed on a slightly ovaloid circle on a small mound which gives it access to an epic panorama of hill-tops – the ancient places of settlement. Whatever else can be disproved, there must have been a fair amount of social cooperation just to haul the stones into place (even more at Long Meg where the Penrith Sandstone would have had to be brought across the river). You can stand in the middle of Castlerigg and be within waving or signalling distance of 1,000 possible habitations of those times. At the very

34

Great Gable mirrored in the deepest and wildest of all the lakes – Wast Water.

The Langdale Pikes from Lingmoor Fell.

Coniston Fells from above Grasmere.

Skiddaw, the oldest rock in the Lake District.

The Screes, Wast Water, 'like the inverted arches of a Gothic cathedral. . . .' Norman Nicholson.

The silver-grey Carboniferous Limestone of Whitbarrow Scar near Grange-over-Sands, an echo of shallow, tropical seas which covered the Lake District some 300 million years ago.

Buttermere.

The lonely and mysterious Swinside Circle, overlooking the Duddon estuary.

least, the circle was made to be widely, comprehensively seen.

My guess is this. The two things most necessary to a hill-dwelling scattered society which was both mechanical (with stone axes/pottery/knife making) and property owning (farming/herding/jewellery) would be a place for commerce and a place for law. The stone circles would serve as a focal point for commerce – their prominence ensures that. They could also serve for a meeting place of law. A megalith for each of the greater men, the open space for disputation or combat. Failing a religious explanation – and there seems nothing to indicate any religious conceptions whatsoever – the grand dignity of these places must have called out to something beyond convenience: the law, it seems to me, would have been the primary reason for existence.

4

After the Beaker People came the Celts. So bound up in poetry and song, so often claimed by myth and legend, the Celtic people, the 'Cymry' (meaning the Compatriots), gave their name to the place – Cumbria. They came into a region, even a culture, which, in the warmer climates of that Early and Middle Bronze Age, found its inspiration in Ireland. Curraghs would swan across the Irish Sea, to the Isle of Man, to Wicklow: there are similarities in the axes, spearheads and daggers. The cairn fields have similarities with those in Ireland – these can be traced at Caldbeck and Crosby Ravensworth for example. With the placidity of the stone circles and the intercourse (suggesting lack of fear; lack of conflict) between Ireland and the North-West, there is the feeling – admittedly a useless

43

The signature of prehistoric man on the landscape: the enclosures at Aughertree Fell near Ireby. The site requires detailed excavation but it is probably Iron Age in date; certainly the oval enclosure on the right bears remarkable similarities to the settlement at Risehow near Maryport.

guide for a professional historian – of a pacific civilization which had overcome the problems of survival without running into the difficulties of organizing diminishing resources.

It seems that the Celts arrived in the second or third century BC from Yorkshire.

Although the natives were already acquainted with iron, the Celts brought in the Iron Age with more sophisticated techniques. They also went in for mixed farming – a definite advance on what had gone before – and they bred and trained horses for riding. They are very likely to have had a powerful religion for, unlike the inhabitants, who were cremated, the Celts were buried in full dress, ready to enter into the next world. I would guess that they appropriated the stone circles for their religious ceremonies – hence the tales of Druids. Their place names persist in the north of the district – Derwent and Blencathra are Celtic – but we know little of the language. Some substantial objects have been found which can claim to be Celtic – most notably the great iron sword in an engraved and enamelled bronze sheath found at Embleton – again interestingly in the northern part of the district.

44

Risehow, Maryport. Here the crop marks indicate a circular or 'banjo' farmstead, probably Iron Age in date.

The most considerable remains of the Celts are the round huts and the hill forts. At Wolstey Hall near Silloth and at Risehow, Maryport, pre-Roman oval enclosures have been discovered, by aerial photography. They are made of stone, occupy sites later re-used by the Romans and point to a firm tribal domesticity – the first evidence of this in the history of the Lakes.

More spectacular are the hill forts: indeed it is difficult to think of anything (man-made) more spectacular in the whole of the Lake District than these fortresses set on the top of rock. Castle Crag in Borrowdale, for example, stands there in the jaws of that most painted and praised valley, like a savage sentinel and an unassailable redoubt – all ground cleared about its base, easy to defend, daunting to attack. Walk under it and try to work out how you might 'take' it with the resources available at the time. Again and again in these hill forts, the Celts took advantage of natural features and built on what already existed. Most dramatically of all, this is done on Carrock Fell, where the truly gigantic Iron Age fort (800 feet by 350 feet) shelters behind a northern wall of natural rock which puts to shame the walls of even the most monstrous medieval castle. They were used for defence primarily against the Picts from Scotland.

The summit of Carrock Fell from the air. The outline of the largest Iron Age hill fort in Cumbria can be clearly traced.

By the time the Romans arrived, the bedrock of the Cumbrian people was laid down. They were farmers and fishermen; they could make great fortresses and fine implements; they were, by the standards of the time, numerous. (Tacitus remarks on their large number.) They had a form of religion which embraced reincarnation and perhaps the beginnings of a system of law. They were the Brigantes, whom the Romans found both tough and shrewd: shrewd enough to make treaties and get on with their own lives; tough enough to break out against the great power when the virus of oppression grew too strong to bear. They were there before the Romans came and when the Romans left they were still there, remarkably intact.

46

The Ill Bell ridge above Troutbeck. The course of the High Street Roman road runs diagonally across the middle distance.

5

The conquering Romans were here for three and a half centuries, and I think a heartening commentary on the inherent strength of occupied Lakeland is that the old life and language continued underground: except that the 'underground' was on the hills.

In AD 90 a division of Agricola's army entered the district below Kendal. Eight years later, Petillius Ceriales crushed the Brigantes. The Romans began to build the roads which would carry their armies swiftly to trouble spots, and forts in which they could house their soldiers. Both roads and forts were constructed to divide and so rule the hill tribes.

A dramatic reminder of hostilities at the Roman fort at Ambleside. The lower inscription on this gravestone reads:

To the Good Gods of the Underworld
Flavius Romanus, Record Clerk,
Lived for 35 years
Killed in the Fort by the Enemy

At Ambleside, Hardknott and Ravenglass, turf and timber forts were built. In Hadrian's reign they were replaced by stone. The road from Ambleside to Wrynose was built – it goes over Wrynose and Hardknott. The road called High Street, from Ambleside to Brougham, was built then, as were routes into the hills from the camps at Old Penrith, Papcastle and Caermote. High Street can still be walked; until a hundred years ago it was still used by drovers. Nowadays you feel on top of the Roman world up there.

Although there appear to be no Roman traces in dialect or place names, the Romans must have made an enormous impact at the time. Not only were they the conquerors; they colonized heavily. They must have needed slaves, food, horses, stone, timber, lead, hide – all of which had to be got locally – and this must have put the domestic economy under great strain at first. Between 192 and 211, Septimus Severus decreed that serving soldiers be allowed to marry: civilian settlements increased, farms and towns seem to have sprung up outside the forts and camps. And there was the contact which came through war, with the inevitable rape, taking of prisoners, looting: a savage method of contact but unarguably powerful. War seems to have been the most regular form of communication between the Romans and the natives. The Ambleside fort (Galava) had to be abandoned for many years after an uprising; throughout the second century the relations between the Brigantes and the occupying forces were strong. But on the whole the Romans got what they wanted in the Lakes; a relatively safe zone. Their real attention was directed to the north and west.

48

The Roman bath-house at Ravenglass which, according to R. G. Collingwood, is the best-preserved Roman building in the north of England.

There is little to be seen of the forts, alas, although many coins have been picked up around the Ambleside settlement; and a bronze bell was found, a bronze eagle, leather shoes, a silver spoon, some pottery. But the prize pieces are at Ravenglass and Hardknott.

At Ravenglass (Glannaventa) there is a bath house outside the fort, which R. G. Collingwood described as 'the best preserved Roman building in the North of England'. The walls are ten feet high; the Roman plaster is still in the stones; and it has of course, attracted its legends. In 1599 Camden was told that King Eveling held his court here; in 1610 John Denton identified it with the Lyons Garde of Arthurian Romance. 'Wall's Castle' it is called – where the ablutions of Rome bred thoughts of courts in later peoples.

On the shoulder of Hardknott Fell stands a fort so splendidly positioned that, as has been said, it seems to be an 'enchanted fortress in the air'. It was occupied from AD 120–38 and again from 160–97. It is 800 feet above sea-level: the view is down Eskdale to the sea, Harter Fell to the south, the Scafell range to the north. Beacons or signal flares gave it contact with Ambleside and the coast. Wordsworth refers to it in the Duddon Sonnets –

> . . . that lone camp on Hardknot's height,
> Whose guardians bend the knee to Jove and Mars . . .

It is square: 375 feet each way, and was capable of housing 500 soldiers. The

49

defensive wall was of stone, about five feet thick; an earth embankment reinforced it. The internal plan is very similar to that at Ambleside: four turrets guard the corners and the main gateway led to the main buildings. There was a granary, barracks of course; the inevitable bath house was outside the walls; and in two of the corner turrets there was a bakery and a forge.

Over the years, local men lifted much of the stone here as they did elsewhere in the district – and throughout Europe, I guess. Recently, though, the fort has been 'restored' by the Ministry of Works and although it looks a bit neat and twee, it usefully represents what once was. If you like the gentle pastime of attempting to immerse yourself in the past, I can think of few finer locations than Hardknott. You can stand with Roman soldiers about their martial business. Not a bad posting, you think on a good day: on a bad, snow-bound or rain-battered day – serve them right!

Of course all this skirts the main testament of Rome just as Rome itself more or less skirted the inner Lakeland. For on the northern boundary of Cumbria is Hadrian's Wall. Suspended seventy-three miles from Wallsend on the North Sea to Bowness on the Solway, this complex system of wall, ditches, roads, forts and milecastles stands as massive proof that the great Romans were indeed here. And from the wall, tumbling down the coast to St Bees there was another system of roads and forts.

In AD 410 the Emperor Honorius signed a document refusing help to the British. The Romans and their dependants were withdrawn. The Romano-British had to fend for themselves against the barbarians whom Hadrian's Wall had been designed to keep out. They were already at the gate and now in they came to begin that almost chartless era known popularly and not unfairly as 'the Dark Ages'. The conquerors pulled out leaving the conquered almost defenceless.

6

I am tempted to take the next six hundred and sixty years as one block. It encompasses the final disintegration of the Roman Empire, the strange story of the Cymry, the arrival of Christianity, the lowland penetration by the Angles and the highland conquests of the Vikings – any one of which could command a volume. But overall there is a single theme: between the end of one great historical block – the Romans – and the beginning of another – the Normans – the locals drew in and digested peoples, customs, habits, rituals and language

The Scafell range from Harter Fell. The Roman fort at Hardknott can be seen in the foreground.

which gave it the particular character it has enjoyed since. In a sense, in those six hundred and sixty years – between 410 and 1070 – Cumbrians went their own ways, subject to no great unifying centralizing ideal (although a prey to many territorial ambitions), and their character was then established.

When the Romans withdrew their protection, we are given to understand that there was widespread devastation by the Picts and the Scots. W. G. Collingwood wrote that it was 'a wonder the local population was not exterminated'.

In 573, St Kentigern, or St Mungo as he is sometimes known, came to Cumberland on a mission from the Celtic Church in Glasgow. It is thought that he preached at Crosthwaite, and a number of churches in the area are dedicated to him – at Caldbeck, Aspatria, Bromfield and Mungrisdale for example. This, the planting of Christianity, was important enough. But the most critical event in Cumbria's history – and, arguably in the history of Western Europe – happened across country in Northumbria where between 593 and 617 Aethelfrith centralized the kingdom of Northumbria and in the process at the battle of

The Bewcastle
Cross, a master-
piece of Anglian
stonecarving.

Cheter (615) drove a wedge between the Welsh and the Cumbrians.

The incalculable significance of Northumbria lay in the protection it gave to a line of Christian missionaries and, perhaps even more importantly, scholars. In the bombed out culture of the post-imperial age, learning had become worn down to such an extent that it has been agreed it hung almost by the single thread of the Northumbrian succession. Had that not held, the actual transmission of information and, more importantly, the tools and languages to decode that information would have been lost. For Bede alone, we have to give thanks; his gift to Cumbria, to the rest of Britain and to Europe, was the wherewithal to begin to connect with the written traditions of the past. Without that we could have been adrift for many more and darker centuries.

Bede, incidentally, wrote nothing of the Cymry before the late seventh century because he considered them an inferior race.

But this united Northumbria, secure in its strength, began to colonize the inferior race, and by the end of the seventh century most of Cumbria was in their hands. Westmorland, incidentally, received its short-lived name here, being called Westmoringaland or the Land of the Western Border of the Anglian Empire.

In 685, St Cuthbert came to Cumbria from Northumbria and got a grant of Carlisle from King Ecgfrith. He founded an abbey and set the main tone of the two centuries of Anglian colonization which was the Christianization of Cumbria. There are none of the early Anglian churches left, but fortunately there are several of the stone crosses and, as our usual good luck would have it, one of the very finest stone crosses of the entire period – the Bewcastle Cross. This, with its heavy ornamentation of vine scrolls, figures, birds, interlace ornament and runic inscriptions, is a mixture of such richness, coming out of Egypt, Greece, Rome, and the zeal of the newly converted of Northern England. What is beguiling, when you look at it, is the wealth of international scholarship that went with it. Here in Cumbria, the symbols and motifs from civilization which had stretched across the known world come together in a masterpiece of stone-carving.

There are other crosses, all pre-875, at, for example, Addingham, Brigham, Carlisle, Dacre, Irton, Waberthwaite, Kendal and Heversham. Later Anglian sculpture can be seen at St Bees, Plumland, Workington and elsewhere. In Penrith churchyard you can see 'the Giant's Grave' which includes some Mercian-influenced crosses.

Inside the 'strict' Lake District there are few early Anglian names. But

52

The Ormside bowl, an
Anglo-Saxon masterpiece in
silver-gilt. Found near Appleby in
1823, it was probably made in
York in the late eighth century.
Dimensions: 5½in. at the rim, 2in.
high.

A thousand-year-old sentinel – the Anglian cross at
Irton.

settlement on land lower than 250 feet is borne out by the early Anglian
place-names ending in 'ingham': (Hensingham, Whicham formerly Whitting-
ham) and the later names ending in 'ham' or 'ton' (Brigham, Dearham, Frizington, Workington, Wigton, Killington – there are literally scores of these: 'ton'
means 'farmstead').

Those of us who write about Cumberland have tended to favour the Vikings.
Our names, often, are Norse in origin. Mine is no exception. The Vikings
actually came into the heartland of the Lake District proper; their spirits did not
fail them in the foothills. They seem to have spliced naturally with the independent rump of Britons still holding the fell-tops – and in fact reinforced the
characteristics of independence and hardiness.

More than that, the place swarms with Norse place-names and the local
dialect – still a potent inheritance from the childhood of most of us – is founded
on the language of the north which must have overwhelmed the vocabulary of
the Britons. It is still an agreeable fact that a journey to Iceland and Norway can
bring you up against a substantial number of words from 'home'.

The Vikings, then, have usually had a sympathetic press from Cumbrians
and long before modern research presented us with the new view – that they
were not at all the horny-helmeted plunderers sent to devastate the peace-loving

A Viking spearhead from Kentmere, tenth or eleventh century.

A Viking sword found at Witherslack.

natives – we 'felt' they were OK. And after all, their history had been written by their enemies.

They made for the very centre of the Lakeland. Tarn (from *tjorn*) is one of their words; so is dale (*dahl*); and fell (*fjall*); beck (*bekkr*); waterfall (*foss-force, falls*); all the manifold variations of 'thwaite' (a clearing or enclosure in the woodland): Braithwaite, Stonethwaite, Rosthwaite, Crosthwaite etc., etc. And the proper names and dialect words are countless. These, too, attached themselves to places in the heartland – Scafell ('bald mountain'), Ullswater ('Ulfor's Lake'), Arnside ('Arni's shieling').

A chief would establish himself in a 'baer' or 'by'. Lamonby – 'the house of Lagman'; Sowerby – the 'sow' farm. His thralls would take cattle and sheep inland and upland for pasture where farms were established. Beyond that would be the summer shielings or cattle farms. Ambleside ('shieling of Amal'). Birker ('shieling among birch trees'). All these were named by the Norsemen and most of those names are in use today. Threlkell ('Thrall's Well'); Grisedale and Mungrisdale – from *griss*, the old Norse name for pig – 'pig pasture'. There are thousands.

From the names, from the dialect and from the customs which persisted for so long (there is a stone in Carlisle Cathedral bearing a Nordic runic inscription), we can take seriously the claim that in the tenth and eleventh centuries Cumbria was the centre of a civilized and settled Scandinavia-West-over-the-sea.

There are very few Viking burials – suggesting that the Norsemen were Christians when they arrived. One or two pagan warrior graves have been found, dedicated to Thor and Odin (one was discovered at Seaton; another at Aspatria), but archaeologically the settlement has proved to be disappointing. Except, yet again, in one gigantic stroke of good fortune which left in Cumbria one of the great memorials of the whole of the Norse epoch – the Gosforth Cross. It is one of the many crosses (others are at Muncaster, for example, and Brigham and Dearham) which show off the rich mixture of Scandinavian and Irish traditions: but the Gosforth Cross is supreme.

It stands fourteen and a half feet high, an elegant sandstone pillar. The lower part is carved to represent the ash tree of Scandinavian mythology – the tree thought to support the world. The squared upper part of the cross has four panels bearing figures illustrating the great epic Edda poem – the *Voluspa*. At the same time they show how the pagan merges into the Christian: Loki, the Evil One, is like Satan; Balder the Good who was killed but said to be promised

54

A silver Viking pennanular brooch found at Orton Scar, dating from the first half of the tenth century. The pin is 11 in. long.

The Norse legend of Thor fishing for the evil world-monster, fossilized in stone in Gosforth church. Thor is on the left, Hymir, the giant, on the right.

The Gosforth Cross, a fascinating fusion of Scandinavian pagan and Christian symbols – a thousand years of digested religion and myth. When it was first erected it was probably brightly painted.

55

rebirth, is represented by a biblical crucifixion. It is as remarkable as it is stunning. A thousand years old, it carries on itself a thousand years of digested religion and myth. Once again, an hour's visit can absorb as much as days of reading.

Meanwhile on the flat lands the battles raged on. Every so often they break the surface of the vague tenth and eleventh centuries like cairns suddenly looking out of a mountain mist. In 945, King Edmund won a great victory and assigned Cumbria to Malcolm, the heir to the Scottish throne, which started a long fuse of trouble. In 966 Ethelred of York ravaged Westmorland; in 1000 Aethelred 'the Unready' ravaged Cumberland. There is evidence that the Vikings tucked themselves into forts (at Tilli near Coniston, at Castle Rocks in St John's Vale), battened down and survived. In 1035 King Knut exchanged Cumbria for Lothian and the border was pushed south. The chief result was that we missed being in the Domesday Book of 1086 which is a great shame. The Scots never did bring us much luck.

By the time the Normans turned their attention to Cumbria, then, it was weathered into a profile whose basic pattern lasted for a very long time. The Norsemen had taken the central highlands, absorbed the Britons and dug in. They were to stay there and they are still there. The lowlands were in flux and beginning to emerge as a vital border area in which battles could be fought and were deemed necessary for territorial sovereignty. The next few centuries would see the highlands harden into a cohesive carapace and the lowlands, especially to the north, be the cause and setting for one bloodbath after another.

7

The Normans were not the last people to invade the district but they were the last people to settle there.

There were battles, of course, but there is persisting evidence, part legendary no doubt, giving the victory to the men already planted in the redoubt of the fells – the Norsemen and the Britons. It may well be so. The Normans made very little impact on the central lands – though yet again we have to face the inglorious possibility that this might have been because they saw nothing worth having there. They got there eventually, though; with the cross rather than the sword.

The Norman barons came north to claim their new inheritance. At the

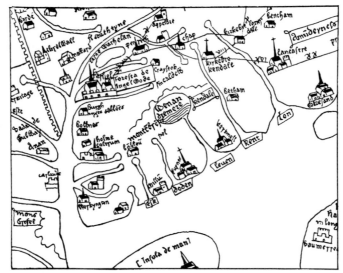

A fourteenth-century picture of Cumbria – part of the Bodleian Map. North is at the left of the map. The major religious houses and important towns are marked, as are the rivers and 'Wenandremere'.

beginning of the twelfth century, for example, Ranulph de Meschines got the land of Carlisle and Appleby. He married the daughter of Ivo Tallesin who had the land of Kendal, and until 1120 Ranulph ruled and reorganized large tracts of the county – though again, mostly the lowlands. In 1120 he was created Earl of Chester and he gave all his lands back to the Crown.

Other baronies were created through the territory; at Allerdale below Derwent, Allerdale above Derwent and the smaller baronies of Gilsland, Liddel, Burgh by Sands and Wigton, to name a few. The famous Bodleian map of 1300 shows up how far the Normans had by then penetrated the district.

They had to defend it of course and it is interesting that yet again – as most famously with the seven cities of Troy – Norman castles rise up on Roman sites. Along the Borders the old sites were used, as at Burgh by Sands, Liddel, Brampton and Irthington – besides Carlisle itself of course. A second line of defence was established at such sites as Cockermouth, Egremont, Appleby and Kendal (which, oddly, boasted two castles: one motte and bailey, and one thirteenth century, stone built). The ruins of several of these castles are still picturesquely preserved. As often as not they belong to the market towns which began to thrive under the farming and productive impulses of the Normans. Markets were established in the twelfth century at Appleby (1110), Egremont (1130–40), Kendal (1189), Penrith (1123), Brampton and Cockermouth (thir-

Egremont Castle, one of the original Norman castles.

teenth century). These, still today the populous buttresses of the main structure of the Lake District, owe the nucleus of their prosperous position to the Normans.

In their daily lives the Normans possibly spent more time and energy on the forests than on the towns. Their passion was for hunting. Its effect on the British countryside – not only in customs but in laws against poaching – was very far reaching indeed. Suddenly the great free landscape became the private park of the ruling classes. All the rest had to suffer for it. No dogs or men with bows and arrows were allowed in the forests; no trees were to be felled; poaching could be punished by death. And all over the land of the lakes ('Cumberland' began to be used in 1177: it could be said that officially the two counties – the other, of course, being Westmorland – began then) these heavily restricted areas were claimed for the conquering huntsmen: Sleddale Forest, Thornthwaite Forest, Skiddaw Forest – there were many but none bigger than Inglewood – a Royal Forest, reserved for the King's hunting and described as 'the most extensive hunting ground in England': forty miles it measured from east to west, twenty-five miles from north to south; and in one day in 1279 Edward I and his friends slaughtered 400 harts and hinds. John Peel's obsession becomes easier to understand.

58

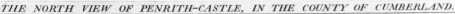

Penrith Castle, part of the medieval fortifications of the Border.

I have left until last what is, in my opinion, the most important Norman endowment to the Lake District: the monasteries. Initially the monasteries were planted in the lowlands: in 1106, a small Benedictine house was established at Wetheral (by Ranulph de Meschines) and in 1120 another was established at St Bees (by his brother William). In 1122–3 an Augustinian priory was set up in Carlisle and, more importantly for the future of the Lake District, in 1127 a Savigniac abbey of St Mary of Furness was established: in 1147 it became Cistercian. It was to become a huge Lake landowner. In 1150, Holm Cultram was founded by Henry, son of David of Scotland, as a daughter house to Melrose: Lanercost was set up in 1166 and Shap, the only one of these inside the fells, was set up in 1200.

But the monasteries soon expanded into the mountain land – some say because the wild and barren land was too much of a handful or too little profitable for the barons. For whatever reasons, the farming clergy pushed into the hills and cultivated them.

St Bees set up chapels at Ennerdale, Eskdale and Loweswater; Carlisle had land in Lorton and Shap; Furness took all land between Coniston Water and Windermere; it also wrested land out of Borrowdale and turned upper Eskdale into a sheep run. Sheep walks, dairy farms, and home farms were the makers of

59

Dacre Castle, an early fourteenth-century pele tower built as a defence against Scottish raids.

this pastoral and pacific invasion, the last and in a way the most lasting in the highlands.

In 1300 French and Latin were spoken, mixing in with the Norse, the abiding scraps of British and Celtic, perhaps a Welsh phrase or two. An organizing ruling class of soldier-administrators had come and conquered and through the forest, the market and the church, layered themselves across the top of the existing society.

8

Apart from invasions by the Scots – which left several pele towers and castles (Dacre, Wythop Hall, Muncaster) and the lovely town of Appleby so devastated, in 1380, that it never recovered – the central massif of the district was no longer threatened. Armies marched past it to and from Scotland until the accession of James I in 1603; even when Bonnie Prince Charlie raised the tartan for the last time (so far) the Lake District was by-passed. The forces of social change which affected the rest of the country worked their effects here too, of course; but after the Normans the place suffered no more serious armies of settlers than those tourists who came to admire and stayed on to live. From the Middle Ages onwards, the flow begins outwards – gathering speed as the centuries march on, gathering force in the two World Wars of this century, resulting in what has been the most consistent export from this area: people.

It had been a tremendous adventure. From Eastern Europe, from the Mediterranean, possibly from Asia, from Scandinavia, Ireland and Normandy, people have come and settled here. All over the county you can see monuments to their occupation. Yet even more moving, I think, is the way in which those disparate races and cultures came together to form such a tight and recognizable society. The men who arrived with their axes in the Langdales, seven and a half thousand years ago, could even now find not only their descendancy but an affinity with the men who still work the uplands and lightly carry the imprint of empires come and gone.

I wrote of this book being in part an exploration. I suppose I could say that reading the history, and visiting and revisiting the castles and crosses and stone circles, gave me some deeper appreciation of what had gone into the background I took for granted. Or that the sense of those others moving through these valleys and hills put a keener perspective on the sort of life led by myself and those I know. Both those would be true – as would be the confession that an understood sense of the past made many an outing since richer in those fragments of thought which drift so idly and pleasantly through your mind as you walk among the fells. But most of all – allowing for the vast increase in comforts and mobility – what I most appreciate is a belief that life here is very like the lives of so many who have gone before. In that sameness there is both security and sanity – consolations, if you like, trivial perhaps at the end of such a span of conflict and struggle – but stabilizing especially now when the possibility of Apocalypse has moved out of religion and into reality.

4

Language

I had originally intended to include language in a chapter which would deal at large with the cultural inheritance of the Lakes and include the legends, the folk traditions, the customs and the sports. The more I read and thought about it, though, the more I became convinced that language deserved a chapter on its own.

For it contains, even now, the unwritten history of more than a thousand years. The Anglians and, much more importantly for our district, the Norsemen who settled here, were not writing men. Their records are to be seen on the hill farms and in the character and lineage of the people. But the fact that people do not write need not mean that their acquaintance with language is limited. The local dialect is proof of that. The number of words and the vivacity of their descriptive power testifies to a most imaginative culture, far away from the glum ignorant silences generally attributed to the fell men. The dialect tells the unwritten story of their ways.

The dialect is largely Norse. There are some Celtic/Welsh words which hung on; there are some Anglian words which are detectable – but these most often elide with the Old Norse which dominates the dialect. The Scandinavian influence spread across the whole of the North of course and Northern English words are also found in Scottish; but Scottish retains more Celtic and has absorbed more French than is found in Northern England.

The language flourished, surviving the Norsemen, avoiding the Latin, finally forced to retreat only by the rise of Chaucer's English. Once England had been determined as a London-dominated and administratively centralized society, then it was clear that a common vernacular would be needed as well as a common official tongue. A single colloquial oral community had to be created. The Southern advance began.

Dating from approximately 1160, this tympanum stone from Pennington Church near
Ulverston bears a Scandinavian runic inscription 'Gamel founded this church: Hubert the
mason built it'. Clearly a Scandinavian script was still in use in the twelfth century.

The remarkable thing is how long the dialect has lasted. For despite the
irreversible advance of Southern English, the dialect was held to for centuries –
a tribute to its usefulness, at the very least.

During this century it has been driven further underground, by the pincer
movement of widespread universal education and the growing genteelness of
English life. Universal education has brought more children to school for a
longer time than ever before and schools have been the traditional enemy of the
dialect. As it is, on the whole, an unwritten language, it offends modern
education in its primary assumption that books are the key to learning. I
sympathize with this but regret that the double tongue, so easily practised by
children who speak dialect on the streets and 'proper' at school, cannot be
encouraged to continue. But from my own experience and that of others, it
seems that the tendency, even the compulsion, is to drive out the dialect not
only at school but in the home. Because, I suspect, to mothers and elder sisters
genteelized by BBC English (a limp latecomer to our language) dialect is not
'nice'; it sounds 'uncouth'; the words are raw, they come from a time of more
direct speech, they are outdoor words in a largely indoor world. The softening
effects of cultivation are steadily at work and what is amiable, inoffensive,
bland, pre-digested and polite is taken to be higher on the scale of things than
that which is rough. It is a sad betrayal of our own past.

Luckily the children – a mixture of outlaws and conservatives – preserve it to
some extent, and over the past hundred years, scholars such as W. Dickinson,

E. W. Prevost, S. Dixon Brown and Robert Ferguson have made successful attempts to put it on paper. The trouble is that it takes a bit of getting used to on paper; it looks very awkward, as if it has forgotten to take off its walking boots and clomped on to the nice clean page too rudely. It demands to be spoken.

The odds are very heavily against it now. In English literature, where a French phrase is thought to be acceptable, where Latin roots sink deep, where Americanisms creep in regardless; where city slang shoulders its way into dialogue and black words are ushered in like guest speakers – dialect is out. The establishment of English literature has never liked it, never tried to understand it, seen it not for its richness but for its comicality at best. The wonderful dialect poems of D. H. Lawrence are still the least known of that great writer's work and perhaps one of the reasons why a continuing clique still resists the claims of his work to be rated with the very best. Thomas Hardy's dialect dialogue has few admirers outside the devotees of Hardy; my own first books, which contained a somewhat diluted dialect, were branded – to some small extent – because of that. It is a pity. We are never so rich that we can turn our back on resources such as there are in the dialects. And in those dialect words, there is not only meaning but history.

In letting the dialect go, in being uncaring about its drift down to children's talk, we have lost a fortune. In this part of the world the hill farmers once again ride in from the past like a cultural US Cavalry to promise a rescue in the final reel. For in their everyday talk, the dialect features strongly. They still use words which provide those fine discriminations which are the glories of language. By losing the words we lose some of our life, to a certain extent, for words carry descriptions of life.

There are so many dialect words that it would test your patience to append anything like a comprehensive list. I would like to end this chapter, though, with a list of words which, in the dialect of these parts, mean **to beat**.

TO BEAT

bang	To strike forcibly producing sound; a heavy blow.
bash	To strike so as to disfigure; includes the ideas of 'batter' and 'knock down'. A blow on some soft yielding matter.
bat	A stroke with the hand, a light blow; a blow from anything falling.
batter	To make sore by repeated blows.

beaste	To thrash with a cudgel; a deliberate whipping judicially administered.
beat	To thrash with fist or stick.
bensal	To thrash severely and repeatedly, say a sturdy lad or truant.
block	To strike with some instrument so as to stun or kill.
bray	To pound; chastise and bruise, mostly in reference to children.
break	To beat with a stick (used chiefly as a threat), generally applied to boys.
buckle	To attack and seize.
bump	To hit the buttocks with the knee.
clap	To pat, fondle.
clapperclowe	To beat and scratch; strike two objects together, implying a sharp strident noise as the result.
clash	To strike violently, generally with something soft; a blow on the side of the head with the open hand.
clattin'	A smart blow on the ear with the fist.
clink	A smart blow on the head and under the ear with the fist or hard weapon.
clonk, clank	A sounding blow on the head.
cloot	A blow with the fist or open hand on the ear, generally severe, and not repeated.
clot	To assault with clods.
clow	To attack and scratch repeatedly.
cob	To kick the buttocks with the broadside of the foot.
corkin'	A very severe beating.
cuff, cluff	A blow on the head given with the hand, less severe than 'clink' or 'clatter' and without malice; also intended as a provocative to a fight.
dander	Same as 'clatter', and 'cuff'.
daud	A blow on the head with something soft, but especially applied to the mouth. To knock backwards and forwards.
deg	To stab.
ding, dang	To knock down and bruise with repeated strokes; a blow which produces a noise.

doon	To throw on to the ground as when wrestling.
doose	A smart slap.
drissin'	Punishment on any part of the body; often means a scolding.
dub	A heavy blow with the fist or head.
dump, dunsh	A blow with the elbow on the side, a butt delivered by sheep or cow.
dust	Used figuratively as in 'dust his jacket', and refers to boys.
flail	To hit with a downward stroke.
flap, flop	A slight blow from the fist, delivered scarcely in earnest, often said of the tongue.
fluet	A very severe castigation; a blow sufficient to knock a person down.
frap	A blow producing a sound.
heft	To thrash unmercifully either man or beast; originally had reference to driving the dagger in up to the heft.
hidin'	A thrashing administered to a boy or girl by the parent.
jab, job	To strike with a pointed weapon; to strike but not so hard as to crush. A slight blow which frightens rather than hurts.
joggle	To strike with a weak uncertain stroke; to shake.
kange	Chastise severely; may also be used in reference to a horse.
kelk	A severe blow delivered by the elbow in the sides or belly with intent to hurt; it may also be given with the hand, knee or foot.
knock	A blow more severe than a 'nap' and often received accidentally.
lam	Punish with the whip; used with reference to a stand-up fight.
larrup	To beat with a strap.
leas	To chastise a boy with a switch.
ledder	To thrash a boy severely, similar to 'bray'.
let slap at	To aim a blow in anger.
lickin'	Corporal punishment of any kind administered to a man or beast.

Daffodils at Gowbarrow Park, Ullswater. 'I never saw daffodils so beautiful. They grew among the mossy stones about and about them, some rested their heads upon these stones, as on a pillow, for weariness; and the rest tossed and reeled and danced, and seemed as if they verily laughed with the wind, that blew upon them over the lake. . . .' Dorothy Wordsworth.

An aerial photograph of the Roman fort at Hardknott. Within the walls the remains of the three main buildings can be clearly identified; from left to right, the unfinished Commandant's house, the Headquarters building, and the stoutly buttressed granary. The wooden-built barracks blocks occupied the ground in front of and behind these buildings. The remains of the bath-house can be seen at the bottom right of the picture.

The twelfth-century Bridekirk font is remarkable not only for its beautiful decoration but also for its inscription in Scandinavian runes which read: 'Rikarth he me wrought and to this glory carefully brought me.' Below this inscription Rikarth himself can be seen finishing his handiwork.

The abbey of St Mary of Furness, built in the local New Red Sandstone.

The village school at Wasdale Head, *c.* 1894. Like many small rural schools, this one has been closed.

lig a leam on	To injure a limb brutally.
lig at, or **in**	To strike generally, and refers to the continuance of the attack, whereas 'lam' refers to the attack itself.
loonder	To thrash in a clumsy manner.
mak at	To rush at with intent to strike or wound.
mash	To bruise, disfigure by blows.
massacree	To all but kill.
nap	To break with a short swift stroke as when breaking stones; a smart blow with the fist or a stick on the head or hand.
neval	A slap.
nointin', ointin'	The punishment which the schoolmaster gives to the scholars, evidently with 'strap oil'.

nope	To strike on the head.
nub	A push with the elbow in the side, but not so severe as a 'dunsh', but used rather for calling attention than giving pain.
paik	A very severe beating given by the schoolmaster. 'Paiks' is also said of a continuance of blows whereby a person becomes exhausted.
pash	To beat with force, pound heavily.
pay	Any form of punishment administered for the correction of a fault committed by a child. To settle a grievance by beating.
peg	A beating less severe than a 'paikin', generally with the fist.
pelk	To strike with force; the blow from a long and moderately thick stick.
pelt	To throw stones at anything; blow on the skin.
powse	A slight blow on the temples. To pull the hair.
prick, prod	To wound with a spear or sharp pointed instrument.
pummin'	A severe thrashing with the fists.
punch	To kick with the foot.
quilt, twilt	To beat keenly.
rozzel	Used rather as a threat than to describe any special form of chastisement; the actual meaning being to apply rosin.
scaitch	To thrash with a stick or rod.
scop	To hit with a stone thrown by the hand or sling; to hit with the fist.
scowe	A 'skelp' emphasized.
settle	To quiet a person by thrashing.
skelp	A smart blow applied by the mother's open hand on the child's bare buttocks.
slaister	To beat severely and disfigure, but without producing serious injury.
slap	To beat with the open hand.
slash	To wound with a cutting instrument.
slough	A blow clumsily struck.
smack	Same as 'skelp' but on any part of the body.

souse	Obsolete and the character of the blow now unknown.
spank	Same as 'skelp' but on any part of the body, and less severely than 'noint'.
stirrup oil, strap oil	Chastisement given to a child with a leather strap similar to that one used by a shoemaker to hold his work firmly on his knee.
strop	To beat with a strap.
switch	To beat with a rod or switch.
tan	To belabour the body.
tap	A sharp stroke on the head.
targe	To beat very severely, almost wounding.
thump	A hard stroke on the fist.
tig	To touch lightly; a very slight blow.
towel	To beat with a stick.
trim	To whip a child.
troonce	To thrash deliberately as a punishment.
twank	To beat with a stick, similar to 'welt'.
warm	To beat, but especially said of children; these last four are very akin to one another in meaning.
weft	To beat generally.
welt	To thrash a grown-up person with a strap.
whale	To beat severely man or beast with a cudgel.
whang	To flog with whip-thong or strap.
whap	To flog with whip-thong.
whelk	A thump with a fist; a severe sounding blow.
whezzle	To beat with a hazel.
wipe	A back-handed blow.
yark	A blow with a heavy cudgel; the use of the word has reference to heavy and severe impact.
yedder	A severe blow with a supple stick or yedder.

Aren't they marvellous? Surely we cannot lose all this. They leap off the gagged page – demanding to be tongued. If we had replaced them – then a sad farewell would be understandable. If we did not need them – again we could forget. But neither case applies. They are there to be lifted from the page and used. Must they finally die of neglect?

Ullswater from above Howtown.

5

Work and Society

1

Most of those who have inhabited this district for the past seven thousand years have farmed it. The land they have had to work is, on the whole, poor. Some farmers have had the good luck to inherit or acquire rich valley soil; for most, the biggest fraction of their portion is fell land which has to be cleverly nursed even for minimum grazing. It is this continuity which attracts me to the hill farmers and labourers.

For so many hundreds of years, so little changed. Although my grandfather lived in a stone-built cottage, his basic accommodation was not very far removed from the small timber hut of the Norsemen a thousand years before; nor were these huts too different from the houses of pre-Roman man. The food would have been more similar than different; oatmeal, milk, cheese, bacon, innards, occasional game and fish (probably much less of that in my grand-father's day due to the scarcity of game and the laws protecting it), few fresh vegetables, a little fruit. Clothes would not be home-made but they were often locally woven. Utensils were few. Travel was restricted chiefly to where your legs would carry you. The day's plan matched the sun's rising and setting. The last fifty years has changed a great deal of that – but the traces remain; a thrifty sense of the subsistence-past endures.

It was the monks who turned farming into an industry. They established fell-sheep ranches. On the back of that they instituted the woollen industry and to complete their hand they developed fisheries. In 1240, the Furness monks were granted 20 nets on Windermere and Thurston (Coniston) Water.

It was the monks who established formal education here and when the monasteries were dissolved in 1536–40, that, too, alongside their agrarian industries, collapsed. Grammar schools reclaimed the ground – Penrith (1564),

A Lakeland farmstead, Wasdale Head.

Kirkby Stephen (1564), Keswick (1566), St Bees (1583), Hawkshead (1585), Kirkby Lonsdale (1591). Chapels were built to meet religious needs; Wasdale (1552), Ennerdale (1543), Wythburn (1552). And market towns from Ulverston in the south to Wigton in the north became – as they remain – the focal point of the farming industry which the Cistercians had organized on a larger scale than ever before. The yeoman farmer took over from the monks but he went to market towns, not to the monastery.

One industry which continued to thrive uninterruptedly was wool. Particularly around Kendal and its twenty-four surrounding townships where fast streams, local dyes (the Kendal Green) and soft water perfectly suited the work. Catherine Parr, who was born in Kendal, gave Henry VIII 'a magnificent coat of Kendal cloth' when she became his (sixth) wife.

Though agriculture continued to be the basic industry, it does not seem to have thrived particularly well over the next three hundred years for when Arthur Young, the scientific gentleman farmer, came to the district in the

Hand threshing of grain with a flail continued in some parts of the Lake District until the 1930s.

eighteenth century he gave it the worst report in the land. He found that the local men had no idea of correct rotation or stock management; he was astounded to see that the biblical rowan plough drawn by oxen was still being used; he found no wheeled vehicles in the uplands and, once again the biblical connection, threshing was still done with a flail.

It was a time when several of the local gentry were trying to modernize farming. Philip Howard of Corby Castle introduced 'Turnip' Townsend's rotation system into the county, and there were John Christian Curwen and Sir James Graham (who introduced tile drainage) – just three of the men who seemed to combine enlightenment with philanthropy – many of them lost money and found their innovations slow to catch on here.

The second important single event after the monasteries was the enclosure movement. Common land was taken from the people and divided among the wealthy in the name of progress. Between about 1760 and 1800 the increased population of the cities and then the French wars created a greater need for food and the landowners seized what had been common to all. With rights of grazing, planting, cropping and wood gathering gone, most of the very small farmers

Gathering sheep for dipping, Ennerdale.

and labourers were forced to seek hire or go elsewhere. In that sense, the dry-stone walls, which literally enclosed the land, would have been seen as so many tombstones by the men ejected from holdings they must have felt had been held freely from time immemorial.

In the nineteenth century, although there were boom times, the actual life of those on the land altered very little. Some farmers grew rich and their newish stone houses were plumped out with good furniture; their stables held one or two hunters; there would be a pony trap, and parties. But it was the mechanization of this present century which gave the third most important jolt to farming around here. Now with tractors, harvesters, jeeps, electricity, scientific fertilizers and the rest, modern farming is a streamlined, efficient, amply subsidized modern industry. The farmers are the new rich; the price of their land alone has put many of them in a bracket of wealth undreamed of. There are few who

A steam threshing machine and farm hands, south Cumbria, *c.* 1920.

A Lakeland clipping *c.* 1880.

A country gathering – the annual Ennerdale Show.

'A bonny l'ile tup'; judging Herdwicks at Eskdale Show.

Broadcasting seed in Great Langdale in the 1950s.

One of the last Cumbrian 'hirings', Carlisle, December 1945. Seventeen-year-old Robert Simpson is hired by Mr Soulsby while his mother looks on to see fair play.

grudge them the luck.

For still they are out lambing in the middle of the night, prey to weather, diseases and the caprices of the E E C; still there is no remission from daily grind to keep the crops rich, the hedges down, the tools clean, the beasts healthy, the milk pure, get the hay in, get the barley in, work every hour there is when you have to which is often enough.

They give back a great deal to the place, not only in holding the centre firm with real and necessary work, employing men and keeping the land fertile and sound, but in the culture they bring – the markets, the meets, the shows, the dances and pubs and parties. *They* are the longest lasting, the deepest planted and the most cohesive force in Lakeland. If they should go, it would wither away.

81

George Birkett clipping a Herdwick ewe in Little Langdale.

A seventeenth-century yeoman farmer's home – Town End, Troutbeck, near Windermere.

2

Partly because they were so attractive to Cumbria's most affectionate historian – W. G. Collingwood – partly because they seem to have provided the model for Wordsworth's earlier and more dynamic ideas about a good society and partly because they are the ancestors of the hill farmers, the 'Statesmen' deserve a section to themselves.

Their denomination as 'Statesmen' is not found in history books until the late eighteenth century, but these men – in effect exceptionally independent farmers – came out of the Norse conquest. It was the Norsemen who seized and held much of the upland territory and made a society which has a fair claim to being called a republic. The Norman Conquest mortally threatened their independence but, by the twelfth century, we find that the Norsemen had regained their estates. Once again, the intractability of the land must have made deals more sensible in the long run than the imposition of the alien feudal

The impressive date-stone over the door of Hewthwaite Hall, near Cockermouth, built in 1581.

structure. And there is some evidence that the Normans never finally overcame the central fortress of those Lakeland holdings.

However it was, the Cumbrians – as they had then become – succeeded in the battle for the land. They extracted special conditions. They had their services fixed, for example – they were not bound by a total oath to their Norman lords whereby he could claim all they had. The only exception was for a Border war when they had to turn over all their men and all their horses. Perhaps even more importantly they established virtual freehold rights in their property – very rare indeed within the feudal system; when a man died, his holding automatically went to his widow and his eldest son or daughter.

James I tried to reduce their power in 1620 and the Statesmen met in Kendal to organize a fund and a petition to Parliament and the King. When that failed and their customary rights were suppressed they took the matter to the Star Chamber, where they won the case. So they could still – as of right – pasture on the commons, for example, and get stone, wood, turf, peat and bracken as they thought fit.

In the previous century – the sixteenth – the Statesmen had grown comparatively wealthy when the price of wool rose by 500 per cent and their rent stayed stable.

This wealth was eventually turned into stone in the 'great re-building in stone'. The finest example of one of the superior Statesmen's houses can be seen at Town End (Troutbeck, Windermere) – built between 1623–6 by George Browne and lived in by his descendants until 1943. There the old oak settles, the chill dairy, the big functional kitchen with its iron and flagstones, the comfortable layout which combines practicality, security and sound tastes – all describe an enviably well-founded civilized life.

84

It is this tradition which lives on in the hill farms today. Few of them are without the most modern amenities; many have old and unostentatiously valuable pieces of furniture; there are few frills but that same solidity and unfussy good taste is there – the grandfather clock, the oak chest inherited, the large dining table often one or two hundred years old, the big fire and the cluttered kitchen, often enough the hams hanging from the ceiling, milk coming in from the byres, pigs butchered on the premises, logs gathered locally, the harvest of careful local living and the traditions of independence in dealing, working and living still maintained.

3

There has been mining of sorts in Lakeland since the man with the axe made his mark seven thousand five hundred years ago. The Romans dug in for copper and lead; silver was found in small quantities and worked throughout the centuries; but it was not until the sixteenth century that the area could boast a substantial mineral industry.

In 1564, William Cecil founded the Company of Mines Royal and a year later about fifty German miners were brought over to start a copper industry in the Newlands Valley. Over the next thirty-five years, £104,000 was invested in this project; the profits were £65,000 and the workings were closed down in about 1650. But two effects came from it; the first was the more ruthless razing of the forest, the second was the employment of local labour at a time when the vacuum caused by the closure of the monastery-based agricultural industry was endangering the future of the entire district. This held people in the district who then re-grouped and went back to the land.

The most continuous industry has been slate-quarrying, which still prospers today. Stone and granite have been quarried for years and they too are still worked, the quarries inching very slowly into the vast hills of rock. Only the graphite industry – particularly in the eighteenth century – compares with the German – copper – enterprise in its heyday. This was based in Borrowdale; in 1788 it was fetching £3,300 a ton and smuggling became another local industry. It was the versatility of this high-quality graphite which made it so valuable. It could be used in the casting of bomb-shells, round-shot and cannon-balls; it fixed blue dyes, glazed pottery, prevented rusting and filled pencils. In about a hundred years the workings were exhausted and nowadays the famous Keswick lead pencils import the lead.

Sixteenth-century mining techniques. Here the ore is being sorted and washed. The main ore-smelting centre for the Mines Royal was Brigham near Keswick.

Here four methods of descending the shaft are shown – A by ladders, B by lowering on a rope, C by sliding down an incline and D by descending steps cut into the rock. Almost certainly these methods were used in the Mines Royal.

The high quality of the minerals was characteristic of the coal and iron ore found on the western rim of the Lakeland – in the case of the coal, often running out under the sea. Once again the rich local families took the initiative and the profits. The Lowthers, Fletchers, Curwens and Senhouses built up (and in one case re-named) the coastal towns of Whitehaven, Workington and Maryport. Humphrey Davey moved there when the Cumbrian coast temporarily threatened to become one of the major industrial centres of Britain and Whitehaven was the third port after London and Liverpool. A steel industry

A fifteenth-century Cumbrian author – a self-portrait of the Furness Abbey monk, John Stell.

Windermere. J. B. Pyne.

Thirlmere and Wythburn. Attributed to J. B. Pyne.

Dr Syntax sketching the Lake. Here Rowlandson caricatures William Gilpin's view of Nature.

Grange-in-Borrowdale. William Green.

Devoke Water, 1853. W. J. Blacklock.

'Ullswater'. Joseph Wright of Derby.

Brandlehow Mine on the shores of Derwent Water, 1862. This was one of the oldest mines in the Lake District and was almost certainly first opened by the German miners of the Company of the Mines Royal in the sixteenth century.

developed which, as I write, hangs on, just; of the scores of pits only one remains; all the iron ore shafts are empty. Atomic energy has now replaced them and for some the great cooling towers of Windscale stand like gravestones over the lives spent on hacking fuel and raw materials from that coastline.

The effect of all this mining on the Lakeland was simple. It drew men off the land and into the pits. The Irish came across – as they have been doing for many thousand years – and Cornishmen came up from defunct tin mines to go down the iron ore mines, which claimed more victims than any other industry. But most of the men came from the hinterland. Once again there are cross-benefits. It kept them in touch with the Lakes, which time and again has threatened to become barren of people – and this connection can still be seen vividly in the Lawrentian connection between the mining villages and the surrounding countryside. The miners and their descendants, then as now, kept hound dogs and whippets, fished, shot, climbed, walked, went back into the place from

Caldbeck bobbin mill.

An early twentieth-century photograph of the interior of the Stott Park Bobbin Mill, Finsthwaite.

George Dawson, one of the last bobbin makers at Stott Park Bobbin Mill. Closed in 1971, the building is now a museum.

which their families had stemmed. This closeness undoubtedly brings a richness to the life of the place even though the coastal rim with its Victorian furnaces and slag heaps seems a world away from the empty natural beauty of the lakeland which borders it.

Other industries in the area have included the bobbin industry – due to the coppiced woodland and the fast pure water (at one stage, southern Lakeland supplied 50 per cent of British bobbins) – and the manufacture of gunpowder. Both these industries – like coal and iron – were characterized by the usual Victorian mixture of inventiveness, skill, entrepreneurial talent, rapacity, exploration, and enormous human oppression, disfigurement, suffering and fatalities.

Industry, then, has come and gone in the Lakes, leaving a few scars after the goods had been taken, serving some solid purpose in providing employment and keeping people in the area, and causing a great deal of change to many of the working population. No doubt when better methods or new world needs are discovered, the hills will again be assailed for the wealth that lies in them. The place is made of mineral wealth and perhaps if that time comes it will be accompanied by a better regard for those local people who will again be recruited to unearth it.

4

It is impossible within this space to give an overall portrait of daily life in the whole of the district. Yet it would be a lack in the book were I not to give some idea of the society which exists there today.

I thought it might be best to write about the village of Ireby, set in the Northern Fells, a truly unspoilt fell village of considerable antiquity with an active history from the Middle Ages and consistent present-day activity.

Ireby squats on the small rise behind Skiddaw, about eight miles north of Keswick; a village of 500 people, a village you could drive through in a minute. There are no tea shops, no souvenir shops, only one shop of any sort in fact and that doubles up as a sub-post-office. There are two good food pubs – the Sun and the Black Lion – a Church of England, now one of a shared 'practice' of three, an 'Old' church, half a mile away, a mark of Ireby's more substantial days, a chapel, a hall, a garage, a police house, a Women's Institute, an infants' school for thirty children, a coal merchant, a small transport firm, a guest house, two carpenters, a builder, a clock-mender, a few 'off-comers' – schoolteachers and salesmen now retired – a Folk Club on Fridays, a billiard and snooker room every weekday and a Cross, which testifies to the day when Ireby was more of a market centre than all the towns around.

Almost all the houses and cottages are on a modest scale, some ingeniously modernized, the few new bungalows, council houses and conversions fitting into the easy two-storey line of the older buildings.

Yet it seems to me – I've lived about a mile away for the last ten years – that the farms which open on to the village streets and those whose land laps around the edges of the place, are what gives the village its pace and tune. When I walk down there in the mornings there is the buzz of the children in the schools, the occasional passage of a car or the infrequent, frequently empty bus, a few men on one of the seats on a warm day – but the hum is from the farm machinery. The cattle come out onto the road to be herded back to the fields; the tractors can and do drive in the middle of the road; sheepdogs dart around corners, probably to avoid the authoritative passage of the Milk Marketing Board's tanker daily filling up from the farms around.

The farms open out to the empty fells which can be seen through every gap between the houses, riding under the sky in a gentle frozen wave of mass.

It is farming talk which dominates the pubs: always such good talk – lambs rescued; a cock among the pigs and found half dead from the struggle; land sold and bought, with all details exhaustively anatomized, prices compared from the different auctions – Wigton, Carlisle, Cockermouth, Troutbeck – horses ready for hunting or jumping or trading; a hundred and one instances of life seen in the fields: a weasel with a robin in its mouth, the rabbits coming back, a fox noted and grimly marked down; hay-timing and harvest anxiously plotted. The weather is cursed and watched for the snatches of fine spells which throw the system into top gear. In the pubs the dominoes go down and the darts bomb into the board, leagues are organized, cricket teams selected or rather rustled up, the men who go down to Wigton to work in the Sidac factory easily slipping back into the life, the women chiefly organizing the committees to raise funds for the school, a charity, a gala day, a sense of harmony. Of course there are divorces, depressions; there is unemployment, failure, bitterness, indolence perhaps and a certain complacency – no different from anywhere else. But the binding grind of the farming life around somehow sweats off the fat. Village life is not thought of as an idyll for nothing: it can be somewhere approaching that – especially when its foundation is in such a tight relationship with the necessities of hard farming.

Every five years, Ireby organizes a fair. The last one took place a few months

Ireby Fair – 'The way we were.' Mrs Bragg. Mrs Wilkinson. Author. Marie-Elsa Bragg.

ago and though it provided a technicolour version of the village, there was, I think, enough of the spirit of the place in it to justify my observations at the time leading me to believe that a village such as this has a sense of preservation and adaptation which is a positive and optimistic indicator for these very uneasy times. It could be said that this might be no more than a rose-tinted view. I would reply that it is based on a fair knowledge of the bleaker side and that it is a reaction not confined to myself but shared, in the general daily or more usually nightly thatch of cheerfulness and common sense which gives the village its character.

As I went down to Ireby Fair

Behind me was Skiddaw clearly anchored in the bright day as fast clouds whipped across the windy sky. Flotillas of fells lay about this great flagship of the northern range. Before me the small plain village of Ireby and as I walked down from Ruthwaite the sound of an accordion squeezed its way through the large country silence.

From this road, the entrance to Ireby is a narrow road between two ancient houses which lean towards each other like confiding sentries. One car can pass

96

Ireby Fair. Women with red kerchiefs, large white pinnies, and
red clogs danced for all the world like the girls at the beginning
of Polanski's *Tess*.

Ireby Fair – stove pipe hats, crinolines, Edwardian neckerchiefs and knickerbockers, bonnets, parasols and black tails; the village dressed up and slid into the past.

through it at a time but once through it – there is the village square, the pub, the hall and the bench or two for sober talk. As I came towards that narrow entrance, the feeling that I was in a film nudged its way forward. Through those two leaning houses I glimpsed a crowd – as I had expected; it was Ireby Fair – but what was this? Stove pipe hats, crinolines, Edwardian neckerchiefs and knickerbockers, bonnets, parasols and black tails; the village had dressed up and slid into the past as easily as pie.

I came into the square and the traditional airs, unmasked by the walls, swirled about the old houses as if they had never left them: a dozen women with red kerchiefs on their hair, blue checked dresses, large white pinnies, and red clogs danced for all the world like those girls at the beginning of Polanski's *Tess*. Not all the spectators were in period dress but, oddly enough, the period costume absorbed the rest so that the general appearance of a different time was maintained.

A Cumbrian clogger, Ireby Fair.

But what sort of Time was it, and why did we all like it so much?

It could be argued that it was Victorian without tears. As I walked around the village there were demonstrations of glass-blowing, horse-shoeing, weaving; all of these crafts attracting more passing trade than the silver band in the 'Sun' field – but all of them somehow prettified. The work, the sweat (still seen in the silver band) had gone out of them: the illness and crippling consequences of all those careful old processes had been fairy-wanded away; now it is play. Yet the crafts remain and craft drew in the crowd full of unbemused interest. A young boy of about ten actually danced up and down and clapped his hands as the glass-blower jetted his blue flame and slowly spun his material into new shapes.

Nor were crafts only represented by past skills. There was a stall selling hand-made jewellery, another displaying beautiful miniatures of birds and flowers painted on goose eggs, and Mr Finlay from Morpeth with his walking sticks, their heads elaborately carved out of rams' horns into fish, reindeer, a serpent's head. A traditional craft, yes, but, Mr Finlay told me, over the last

The Furness Morris Men keep alive the age-old tradition of mumming.
Here the pace-egg play is performed in the village square at Cartmel.

year or so, five evening classes had started up in Northumbria – each with twenty to thirty pupils.

Crafts without the pressure of profit, then; is that how we see ourselves? It's useful to ask, because the length and breadth of this country at this time of year people in country villages are dressing up for fairs and carnivals of all sorts and sizes – and in all of them there is the dream of how we would like things to be. Ireby Country Fair was not just a day out – pubs open, greasy pole, melodrama in the Globe Hall at night and dancing and drinking after *The Murder in the Red Barn* – it was a time when people set out their stalls to suggest the sort of life they wanted.

That was why it continued to be like being in a film. The spectators were watching each other to see how they reacted to this *mis-en-scène*. 'Lovely atmosphere' . . . 'It suits him, that hat' . . . 'It was my grandmother's' . . . In 1981, then, this is how a portion, perhaps even a representative portion of people in the approaching society of the silicon chip, want things to be – and see their culture as being able to provide it.

Craft-based. Things that take time to learn but can be learnt, that are difficult to do but can be done and in themselves have something of wonder when they

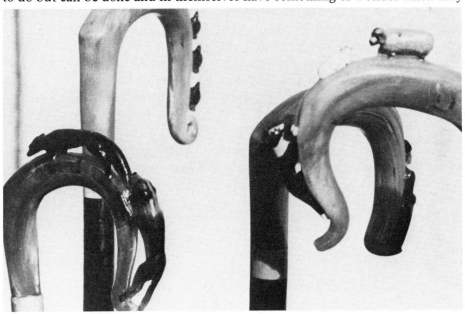

Shepherds' crooks and sticks at Eskdale Show.

101

are done superlatively well. The urge and the willingness to retreat into ancient crafts in order to carry on contemporary life seems strong and widespread. And people were pleased, as they said, to see so many youngsters in the Cockermouth Mechanics Silver Band: it took time to master the cornet and the girls were as many as the boys.

In this sense, the folksy-hobby aspect of the various craft stalls stops being merely quaint. Perhaps this return or regression is a fertile response to the collapse of so many of the bigger and craftless ways of making things and money. With factories falling like rain all over the north, we now have little left but brains and skills: to see such a flush of activity is, in my opinion, more than a straw in the wind. People wanting to make things to a high standard for their own satisfaction and finding an admittedly as yet local market could be pointing a way. It's agreeable and perhaps not so wishful to think that the way out or up or forward might for the future be through the making of beautiful artefacts.

There was also a common sense of the worth of preserving the past. Those period costumes, unselfconsciously worn and so easily adapted, demonstrated that people were glad to belong to the place, to love its past. Perhaps this is far more potent in the country than in the city – but this sense of seeking for a rapprochement with history could well be an indicator that the trough of post-imperial blues might be over. The sense of settling for what we have and relaxing into it could be the most healing pointer imaginable.

There were seven groups of Morris dancers, and a magnificent hot air balloon – a Gulliver of Technology towering over the Lilliputian cottages – but these, the two principal attractions, were the extremes in a day which chiefly showed off the dreams of the people. The Morris men and women were fine but, as it were, professionally involved in the past; the balloon was a wonder (how did the flames which heat up the air not set it alight?) but it could have come from the moon. The daily round was in the craft of doing and making things well.

I'm sure this is by no means an isolated case. Even within that small area of north Cumbria there was a carnival on the same afternoon six miles away at Aspatria with magnificently worked floats and, just a few fields off, the local children's day at Uldale. Is it too much to see in this quiet care and undeniable surge of interest in what can be well turned by an individual, a glimpse of where our misdirected, mismanaged and mangled national energy might be going? As an expression of the cultural values of the few hundreds who turned up, the conclusion is undeniable: skill, care, expertise, difficulty and individuality are what are prized; and being exercised.

Arthur Irvine of Boot in Eskdale is famous for his fine shepherd crooks.

A few years ago I would have dismissed such a display as being part of that phoney, maypole wallowing well satirized by *Lucky Jim*. But things have changed. People have seen the rainbow's end. The boundaries have shrunk, the walls are higher. On a thoughtful day at Ireby Fair you could see and be quietly optimistic about the response to all that.

Millican Dalton, one of a long line of Lakeland eccentrics, seen here on his home-made raft, the *Rogue Herries*, sailing on Derwent Water. A dropout from twentieth-century pressures, he died in 1947 aged eighty.

6

Sports

1

The Lake District has enjoyed the usual national sports – in a more than usual degree, it seems, judging by a pronouncement in 1656 which said 'These Counties of Cumberland and Westmorland have been hitherto as a proverb and a by-word in respect of ignorance and prophaneness. Men were ready to say of them as the Jews of Nazareth – Can any good thing come out of them?' This censure was a result of too much attention being paid to 'shooting, playing at football, stool ball, wrestling'. Some would say it still goes on.

There is football here, of both varieties; cricket, bowls, tennis, squash, swimming – all the national games. What is special to this area though is wrestling, fell-racing and hound trailing. While it would be unthinkable to write a book on Cumbria without mentioning hunting.

2

Cumberland and Westmorland wrestling is in many ways the most interesting and, to any prepared to watch carefully, the most rewarding of all the local sports. At first sight it seems very odd. Men in singlets and long johns wearing black velvet swimming-trunks, often as not embroidered front and bum with silken flowers, black stockings, no shoes, come up to each other and after a handshake, slump their head down on the other's shoulder and nestle there, apparently content. Meanwhile, like the languid legs of an octopus, four arms flail about in slow motion occasionally landing on a back. Eventually a grip is established and then another grip. Instantly the cuddly loose-jointed crab-dance stiffens and shudders into life as the two men twist and swivel for advantage. Should the grip be broken or any part of the body but the foot touch

Hexham Clarke (in the flowered trunks) and the indefatigable George Steadman in action at Grasmere Sports. Steadman retired in 1900 aged fifty-four having won the heavyweight category at Grasmere on seventeen occasions.

the ground, the bout is over. In some ways – in the length of preparation compared with the speed of the actual combat – it is not unlike Japanese wrestling – and perhaps almost as impenetrable to foreigners. But it has been here for a long time – best seen at Grasmere or Ambleside sports or at any of the smaller meetings – and is most unlikely to die out.

Some people say that this is Graeco-Roman wrestling brought by the Imperial armies about 2,000 years ago; others claim it, yet again, for the Norsemen – and there is an almost identical sport in Iceland.

In 1256 William of Gospatrick had his shin broken by David de Brugings in a wrestling match; there's a book of 1581 by Richard Muncaster which refers to it; legends are plentiful; there's Hugh Hurd, 'The Troutbeck Giant', who is

106

said to have beaten Edward VI's wrestling champion in London. Better authenticated figures include the Reverend Abraham Brown who seems to have enjoyed a not uncommon conjunction of the cloth and the sport, and John Woodall of Gosforth, said to be the strongest man known.

In the nineteenth century it became the fashion and in 1851, for example, there was a 'world championship' wrestling match for the very handsome purse of £300. It was won by Robert Atkinson of Sleagill. Perhaps the most substantially famous figure though was George Steadman of Asby near Appleby who retired in 1900 aged fifty-four having won the heavyweight category at Grasmere on seventeen occasions.

Cumberland and Westmorland wrestling has its own terms to describe the holds and grips. A 'hype' is where you lift your opponent, then strike inside or outside his knee. Inside for 'inside hype'; outside for 'outside hype'. A 'buttock' is where you get your buttock under your opponent's stomach as a fulcrum and throw him bodily over. A slack hold is the best for this and held just below the neck is most effective. A 'hawk' is where you get your leg twisted round your opponent's so that he cannot free it. Then, by twisting and lifting simultaneously, you can force yourself over him so that he has to fall over. A 'cross click' is where you click your opponent's heel with your left heel. You pull his leg towards you at the same time and throw your chest forward. Those are just a few of the holds.

For me, the most unusual man to come out of all wrestling is William Litt (1785–1847). He was meant to be a clergyman but preferred the outdoor life. He took up farming and, because of his interest in wrestling, neglected it. He tried his hand as a brewer in Whitehaven and failed at that; emigrating to Canada he failed to make a living writing for the newspapers and ended up a teacher dying before his time, we are told out of 'homesickness'.

Clearly he was entranced by wrestling and the status of wrestler which he desperately wanted to upgrade. He would love it today if he could see places called the Kendal Wrestling *Academy*. In his writings on wrestling he was always referring to proven wrestlers as 'scholars'. I find it touching that he should want to take this rough and ready local sport and aggrandize it. Somehow, although he was a local man, I always picture him as rather a lonely man, hovering about on the edge of things, wanting to justify his lonely passion by giving it class. He used to wrestle in his top boots – much disapproved of by the writer Christopher North who otherwise found him an 'honest, upright, independent Englishman'. He was, it seems, a good wrestler.

In his determination to give the sport a pedigree, he went back to the Old Testament. Perhaps it is merely ridiculous – this reaching out for respectability. But there is something in it too, something in the feeling that strikes you, now and then, when two men come on to a stretch of ancient turf, shake hands and wrestle. It seems indeed to come out of the earliest times and speak of struggle, play, not war but necessary conflict – and man to man, no weapons, no artificial aids. Here's William Litt in his book *The Origin of Wrestling*.

We find in the 32nd chapter of Genesis, that Jacob having passed his family over the brook Jabbok, was left alone. In its history of events at this early period of the world, with a brevity commensurate with its high importance, the Bible minutely relates only those particular occurrences which refer to some covenant, or promise, then made, renewed, or fulfilled. It narrates facts, without commenting upon them. Therefore, although Jacob's wrestling with the Angel was too remarkable an incident to be omitted, yet we are not told in what manner he came, nor of any preliminary conversation or agreement between them. It however appears very evident that until the Angel manifested his miraculous power, Jacob believed his opponent was a mere mortal like himself; and on whichever side the proposal originated, it was acceded to by the other, either as a circumstance not unusual, or as an amicable amusement, which might be practised without the least infringement on cordiality. If it was not unusual, we are warranted in supposing it a common diversion antecedent to that period, and that Jacob was himself a scientific practiser of the art when he was the father of a large family. Nay, we might even *hint*, his celestial opponent was himself no stranger to that athletic amusement. If it *then* had its origin, no admirer of this athletic science can wish for one more ancient, or more honourable. That the Patriarch's antagonist was a being of a superior order, and sent by Divine authority, no Christian has ever yet disputed. That it was a corporeal struggle, or *bona fide*, a wrestling match between them, is universally admitted. It cannot therefore be denied that it is either of divine origin, or that a Being more than mortal has participated in it. It is true, many of the commentators dwell upon it as a *spiritual*, as well as a *corporeal* struggle; this we are very ready to admit; but we will at the same time contend that, instead of diminishing, it adds considerably to its splendour. An amusement from which so many inferences and conclusions have been drawn to promote the welfare of Christianity cannot be either degrading, or confined in its nature; but on the contrary, noble and scientific.

3

Hound trailing is as parochial as Cumberland and Westmorland wrestling but far far younger. It is very much the sport of the 'ordinary' man – and a trip to a hound trail will bring you into contact with as large and easy a group of locals as anywhere you can go.

On every weekday evening in a field somewhere in the Lakes, throughout spring and summer, men, women and, sometimes, adolescents, stand in a long line or crouch, each holding a dog by the scruff of its neck. The dog is lighter than a foxhound but with enough of the foxhound's character to keep the hunting connection warm. A man will trot towards them, having walked five miles dragging a rag soaked in oil and aniseed; when this sport began, late in the nineteenth century, it was a freshly killed fox which was dragged across the

The 'slip' or start at a Lakeland hound trail, Lowick.
Essentially a sport for the 'ordinary' man, hound trailing has
taken the place of the once-popular cock-fighting.

earth. Aniseed and oil have a stronger scent. The handkerchief will be dropped by the starter; the dogs released; then they'll bay and yelp and gallop off for a ten-mile race which they will finish in about thirty minutes.

After they have gone, a second man will come in with his soaked rag from the direction from which the dogs will finish. He and the first man, both called 'Trailers', have met five miles out and each walked a lonely rural semi-circle of fell-land with the soggy rag trailing behind them. When the dogs are sighted – often on the breast of a fell – the owners will set up a cacophony of whistles, shouts, threats, calls – all urging in their hounds. It's a betting sport and the gambling can be serious.

Much of the care that goes with the maintenance of a hound is to do with its food. Secret recipes are passed on from father to son, as they were for the fighting cocks which once thrived over all Cumberland and Westmorland. It is a dubious distinction that the North, particularly the North-West, enjoys of being the place in which cock-fighting, so passionately beloved of Henry VIII and James I, was so devotedly followed. But it was. Now at the broader end of the social scale, hound trailing has taken up the popular following once enjoyed by cock-fighting.

Reminders of cock-fighting lie all over the county. The best 'natural' ring is probably that in Stainton, in Furness. There's a scooped saucer hollow in the village green containing a flat platform about seventeen feet in diameter which is surrounded by a ditch. The privileged few – the owners and handlers and local gentry – could squat in the ditch to watch the finer points as the steel spikes – called 'spurs' – lashed out rapidly. The other spectators stood outside the outer ring; and gambled of course.

There are cockpits all over the area and one of the peculiar things about them is their proximity to the church or the school. Clergymen often presided at cock-fights and in some villages they took place after Sunday morning church. In the local schools, the connection between scholarship and cock-fighting established in London under Henry II continued until well into the nineteenth century, with pupils paying the master a 'cock penny' to provide a prize for cock-fighting or to supervise it.

'Mains', as cock-fights are known, were held in the fells and dales for at least a hundred years after they were made illegal in 1835. Unlike bull-baiting and badger-drawing, which were made illegal at the same time, the attraction to fighting cocks proved adhesive. Indeed, I can remember being shown fighting cocks when I was ten or eleven – thirty years ago – and by sly nods and whispers

– later confirmed – given to understand that it still 'went on'. It does yet, some say.

Fortunately, perhaps, hound-trailing shows all the signs of providing satisfaction to the same animal/sport/personal involvement obsession. Owning one of those dogs is as inexpensive as owning a fighting cock was a hundred years ago. Fortune guarantees that no one can be looked down on; qualities like speed of foot and strength of strike cannot be legislated for even with secret recipes – and so the chances are open. Around the towns and villages, the man who has trudged the lanes for years with his beloved 'triers' and 'also rans' can suddenly become King of the Castle.

The blood-letting side of local sport continues only in fox-hunting. There are those for it, those against it and those who are indifferent to it. It cannot be denied however, that foxes are a serious pest and, if unchecked, would hasten many a local farmer on to ruin. Given that, the defenders of the sport maintain that hunting is the most efficient and least barbarous method of culling. Certainly before fox-hunting became the fashion – in about the middle of the eighteenth century – the other methods appear devastatingly cruel. Steel traps, fox screws, and goose bields (trapping a fox which would then die of slow starvation) appear no better alternative than the chase. Nor does the uncertain nature of shooting – with wounding always a strong possibility – seem attractive. Nothing does.

There are two distinguishing features of Lakeland fox-hunts; the nature of the humans involved and nature itself. The terrain dictates hunting on foot in the central part of the Lakes – the hills, gullies, gorges, ghylls, passes, screes and rocks – mean that men on foot, with strong legs and an acute sense of direction, can tack and cut across the countryside behind their pack in a way which would be forbidden on horse. The people who follow the hunt in this district are fit for it. There is nothing of the scarlet-coated stockbroker in these hunts. The sport is sustained, again, by local men, generally farmers, their families, and the labourers who are well able to keep up the stiff pace. And as many of those who follow the sport like to hunt on horse as well with one of the packs around the skirts of the fells, it is generally the farmers who can afford the horses and they again who form the central core.

There have been many legendary huntsmen here as in every other part of the country. Hunting seems to be followed by fanatics and fleshed by epic characters. The twin counties have their share with Dixon of Kentmere; Tommy Bowman who hunted continuously with the Ullswater pack from 1879–1924;

112

'From the view to the death in a morning' . . . A fine dog fox.

The hunting horn competition, Eskdale and Ennerdale Puppy Show.

Tommy Dobson who founded the Eskdale and Ennerdale Hunt in 1857 and served it until 1910; and the most famous huntsman in all literature – John Peel.

John Peel's wider fame comes from a song dashed off in a few minutes to a Scottish air by his friend John Woodcock Graves of Wigton. The song was first sung in the pub in Caldbeck. It is a simple account of Peel and his life. 'D'ye ken John Peel with his coat so grey'; grey because it was woven of the local wool; it lists his dogs: 'Ranter and Royal and Bellman as true'; it refers to one or two of the places on his routes: 'From Low Denton Holme up to Scratchmere Scar', and it has a rousing refrain. 'Twas the sound of his horn brought me from my bed/And the cry of his hounds has me oft' times led . . .' Simple stuff – yet it has been played in war and peace, in dance halls, and open fields wherever men have gathered to hunt. No matter that another song about Peel – 'The Horn of the Hunter is silent' – is arguably better verse and certainly more topographically detailed: John Peel lives in 'D'ye ken John Peel'.

He appears to have been worth the legend. Stories of his driving his dogs fifty

113

John Woodcock Graves, who wrote the words of 'John Peel', emigrated to Tasmania. This manuscript copy, in his own hand, is dated Hobart Town, May 24th, 1866.

miles in a day are common; he loved his drink; his passion for hunting made him neglect farming and family in the spirit well known to zealots or epic heroes. He hunted on the day his favourite son died and brought back a fox's brush as a tribute. And he incorporated something of the independent, free-ranging, Viking qualities which so many of those who have written about this area – and not all, by any means, romantics – see as the spinal cord of the Cumbrian body. There's this serviceable, plain description of him by Jackson Gillbanks (who wrote 'The Horn of the Hunter . . .').

John Peel was a good specimen of a plain Cumberland yeoman. On less than £400 per annum he hunted at his own expense, and unassisted, a pack of foxhounds for half a century. John has in his time drawn every covert in the country, and was well known on the Scottish borders. Except on great days he followed the old style of hunting – that is, turning out before daylight, often at five or six o'clock, and hunted his fox by the drag. He was a man of stalwart form, and well built; he generally wore a coat of home-spun Cumberland wool – a species called 'hoddengray'. John was a very good shot, and used a single-barrel, with flint lock, to the last. Though he sometimes indulged too much, he was always up by four or five in the morning, no matter what had taken place the night before; and, perhaps, to this may be attributed his excellent health, as he was never known to have a day's sickness until his last and only illness.

A sport which is again, like the wrestling and the hound trailing, particular to the Lake District, is fell running, or the Guides Races as they are now known. It is simple: you run to the top of a fell and back down. Even watching it is hard

114

Successors to John Peel; the Coniston Foxhounds setting off for the first draw at the Troutbeck Mayor's Hunt.

115

A sport for the fittest – a fell runner at Ennerdale Show.

work as you crane your neck to see the diminishing runners climbing the fell face and then glance desperately at the same spot as they come bounding and crashing down as if an avalanche were on their heels. The swiftness of the enterprise is daunting; I was at Grasmere sports a few years ago when a young man called Reeves went up and down a fell in about twelve minutes. It would have taken twelve minutes for most of us in the sports arena to have reached the east gate. A development of this sport has been stamped on the national consciousness by the remarkable Wasdale shepherd, Josh Naylor, who specializes in long treks of endurance. Recently, for example, he ran up sixty-one summits, a distance of ninety miles (the total ascent was 34,000 feet), in twenty-four hours.

To see most of these sports you are often advised to go to Grasmere, Ambleside or Keswick – and, given the weather, you can have a good day. But better by far, I think, is to seek out a small show or a 'meet' somewhere off the central artery of the Lakes; and there, with a strongly local cast, you will see played out the wrestling, running, dog racing and betting which are so integral to life in this area. While afterwards there will be a greater chance of finding a pleasant pub to enjoy the other unfailingly pleasurable sport which rounds off the day.

7

Legends and
Traditions

There is something about legends, nowadays, which does not resonate as we imagine they used to. Perhaps we are too anxious for facts. Perhaps in a more self-confident time – as happened in the nineteenth century – the legends will ripen again.

The place is full of them. It has all the elements for a first-class legend farm: remoteness; large forces of nature; lengthy historical settlement; tenacious wild life; Celts, Norsemen and more than a touch of the Irish; evangelical early Christianity and the full complement of paganism; King Arthur and his Knights supposedly riding and reigning about the place; Sir Walter Scott to round them all up into ballads, Wordsworth to give the occasional stamp of authenticity. The Lake District is an elephants' graveyard of legends.

Here are a few of them.

St Herbert the hermit lived on the small island in the middle of Derwent Water in the second half of the seventh century. He was a friend of the great Cuthbert of Lindisfarne and when Cuthbert paid visits to Carlisle (then Luguvalium) Herbert would walk there and reinforce his faith. The simple Herbert made a wish: that he should die on the same day as Cuthbert. This was granted and, to add to Herbert's contentment, he was given a long chastening sickness before his death, as the Venerable Bede reports, 'so that he might be received into the same seat of eternal bliss'. Both men became saints. That island on Derwent Water does have an 'attraction' yet. Wordsworth wrote about St Herbert and it is touching that still today, beside the island, Christians are bodily baptized and reborn into Christ.

There are several legends dealing with St Cuthbert and almost as many describing King Arthur. Some suppose Carlisle to have been his capital. One ballad – 'The Ballad of Tarn Wadling' or 'The Marriage of Sir Gawain' – tells

Derwent Water and Cat Bells.

how King Arthur was threatened by a giant in the forest of Inglewood. He had
to answer a question – 'And bring me word what thing it is/That a woman will
most desire' – or pay a ransom.

A remarkably ugly woman is then introduced into the ballad: no detail is
spared. Picasso would have been overjoyed –

> Then thereas should have stood her mouth,
> Then there was sett her eye;
> The other was in her forhead fast
> The way that she ought see –

She gave the answer after Arthur had – a trifle cavalierly in all the circumstances
– promised the monstrous female the hand of 'gentle Gawain my cozen' in

119

marriage. That was his part of the bargain. Loyal Gawain married her – ugly though she was. He had done the right thing. She turned into a beauty. The giant was thwarted and everything turned out for the best. The answer to the riddle? Very pre-feminist –

> She says a woman will have her will,
> And this is all her chief desire.

Another legend of King Arthur takes him into St John's in the Vale where he is beguiled into an enchanted fortress by Gwendolen, the beautiful witch who kept him from the defence of Britain against the invaders. Needless to add, our hero escaped in the final reel.

St John's in the Vale contains a natural phenomenon known as the Castle Rocks of St John. From a distance they appear the ruins of a massive castellation; they are, in fact, the clustered mossy rubble of fallen rocks. Legends persisted, however, that the rocks turn from enchanted castle walls into mere stone only at the approach of alien humans. The Blessed – such as King Arthur – can penetrate the mystery and discover the 'real' castle. Sir Walter Scott used it in one of his Arthurian ballads – 'The Bridal of Trierman'. Arthur rides out from 'merry Carlisle' past 'huge Blencathra's ridgy back' – 'till on his course obliquely shone/The narrow valley of St John'.

> Paled in by many a lofty hill,
> The narrow dale lay smooth and still,
> And, down its verdant bosom led,
> A winding brooklet found its bed.
> But, midmost of the vale, a mound
> Arose with airy turrets crown'd.
> Buttress, and ramparts circling bound,
> And mighty keep and tower:
> Seem'd some primeval giant's hand,
> The Castle's massive walls had planned,
> A ponderous bulwark to withstand
> Ambitious Nimrod's Power.

The legend of the Phantoms of Souther (or Sourter) Fell was recorded by William Hutchinson in *The History of the County of Cumberland* (1794). It is an example of mass delusion, optical illusion or magic. It began in 1735 when the

The Castle Rocks of St John, the scene of Walter Scott's Arthurian epic 'The Bridal of Triermain'.

servant of William Lancaster said that he saw the east side of Souther Fell being traversed by a vast army. He said that the whole army was well ordered, distinct and in battle formation. Nobody believed him.

Two years later William Lancaster himself observed a similar phenomenon; he called up his family as witnesses and they too saw an army. Interesting and 'convincing' details were related from that occasion. Some years later, on the midsummer eve which preceded the 1745 invasion, twenty-six people saw the army on the march. Bigger this time and decked out with carriages. Various worthy Cumbrians were there and were impressed enough to climb the hill the next morning and look for prints, marks, any physical trace. None were found.

Another apparition is recorded in De Quincey's *Recollection of the Lake Poets*.

He describes how a young lady, a Miss Smith, went, unaccompanied, up beside Aira Force. She lost her way and found herself stranded, unable to move up, back or sideways. Those who have strayed about rocks or cliffs will recognize the predicament. In trouble and a panic she was relieved to see her sister across the gorge. The sister beckoned and guided her on to a safe path and then disappeared. When Miss Smith returned home she found her sister at home – never having stirred from the house. As a psychic experience, fairly common; made romantic because of Aira Force (and of course because of De Quincey).

There was a self-educated man from Cartmel, John Briggs, who became a schoolmaster and something of an antiquarian. Here is his account of the 'spirits' or 'Dobbies' from his part of the world. Tales of such spirits occur all over the district.

According to the ancient sages of Westmorland – the oldest and best acquainted with the philosophy of spirits – no spirit could appear before twilight had vanished in the evening, or after it appeared in the morning. On this account the winter nights were peculiarly dangerous, owing to the long levels which dobbies could keep at that season. Indeed there was one exception to this. If a man had murdered a woman who was with child to him, she had power to haunt him at all hours; and the Romish priests (who alone had the power of laying spirits) could not lay a spirit of this kind with any certainty, as she generally contrived to break loose long before her stipulated time . . . In common cases, however, the priest could "lay" the ghosts; "while ivy was green", was the usual term. But in very desperate cases, they were laid in the "Red Sea", which was accomplished with great difficulty and even danger to the exorcist. In this country, the most usual place to confine spirits was under Haws Bridge (on the River Kent, near Natland), a few miles below Kendal. Many a grim ghost had been chained in that dismal trough. According to the laws of ghosts, they could only seldom appear to more than one person at once. When these dobbies appeared to the eyes, they had not the power of making a noise; and when they saluted the ear, they could not greet the eyes. To this however there was an exception, when a human being spoke to them in the name of the Blessed Trinity. For it was an acknowledged truth, that however wicked the individual might have been in this world, or however light he might have made of the Almighty's name, he would tremble at its very sound, when separated from his earthly covering.

The causes of spirits appearing after death were generally three. Murdered persons came again to haunt their murderers, or to obtain justice by appearing to other persons, likely to see them avenged. In this, however, the spirit seems generally to have taken a very foolish plan, as they mostly appeared to old women, or

Aira Force, the scene of Miss Smith's 'apparition'.

young men, with old women's hearts. – Persons who had hid any treasure were doomed to haunt the place where that treasure was hid; as they had made a god of their wealth in this world, the place where their treasure was placed was to be their heaven after death. If any person could speak to them, and give them an opportunity of confessing where their treasure was hid, they could then rest in peace, but not without. – Those who died with any heavy crimes on their conscience, which they had not confessed, were also doomed to wander the earth at the midnight hour. These three causes are all that we have been able to discover among our Westmorland hills, where the laws of spirits seem to have been extremely well understood. Those spirits had no power over those who did not molest them; but if insulted, they seem to have been extremely vindictive, and to have felt little compunction in killing the insulter. They had power to assume any form, and to change that as often as they pleased; but they could neither vanish nor change while a human eye was firmly fixed upon them.

There are scores of stories of unhappy lovers. Something about this condition greatly appealed to Victorian anthologists who seem to delight in turning up 'ill fated lovers' in every stately pile in the county. You find them at Muncaster Hall where a jealous knight had a 'simple' carpenter murdered because he loved and was loved by 'the lovely Helwise' of Muncaster Hall. Needless to say it did him no good; she went into a convent on Soulby Fell. Meanwhile down in the ruins of Furness Abbey, James and Matilda, having pledged eternal love, were just as unfortunate. He was drowned at sea; she, like 'the lovely Helwise', sought the consolation of religion.

Then there's Charles and Maria – around Walla Crag. Once again, idyllic and pure love; death – this time of Maria despite Charles's devoted nursing; subsequent suicide of Charles on Harter Fell.

There's the Maid of Hadra Scar – the legend of a beautiful rich young lady who came to Hawes in 1807 and gave no name. She lodged with a widow. One evening she went out for her usual walk, did not return and was never seen or heard of again. You would expect legends arising from sudden, unexplained disappearances in a district such as this. Like tales of wild dogs – 'the wild dog of Ennerdale' being the most famous – they come with the mountains.

Castlerigg's stone circle excited many legends including the inevitable Hammer Horror Show or Human Sacrifice with the Druids eventually being thwarted by a good old miracle. In one case, just as the flames were reaching up to consume an unfortunate young virgin – the rocks opened, the water flowed, the flames were doused and the Druids were on the decline.

Mary Robinson, 'the Beauty of Buttermere', and her seducer, John Hatfield *alias* 'the Hon. Colonel Hope'. Sadly he was neither a colonel nor honourable. He was a bigamist and a forger who was hanged in Carlisle in 1803.

Both Wordsworth and Sir Walter Scott wrote of the dog which was said to have kept by his dead master for three months under Helvellyn. His master had fallen off Striding Edge.

> Like a corpse of an outcast, abandon'd to weather,
> Till the mountain winds wasted the tenantless clay.
> Not yet quite deserted, though lonely extended,
> For faithful in death his mute favourite attended,
> The much-loved remains of his master defended,
> And chased the hill-fox and the raven away.

Thus spoke Sir Walter. Laureate William had written –

> But hear a wonder, for whose sake,
> This lamentable tale I tell!
> A lasting monument of words

125

This wonder merits well.
The dog which still was hovering nigh,
Repeating the same timid cry,
This dog had been, through three months' space
A dweller in that savage place.

There was much more, from both bards.

My favourite 'legend' is, in fact, Wordsworth's poem 'Michael' which tells a sad classic story of an old shepherd and his wife deserted by their beloved only son and pining away from grief. There's quasi-legendary history – such as Mary, the Beauty of Buttermere, praised by poets and painters, married by a bigamist and forger who was hanged at Carlisle, while she endeavoured to become respectable in Uldale at the last. There are giants as in Lady Ern the Giant; and sudden wonders – rocks splitting, apparitions appearing, spirits spiriting. All the company of legends hum over the landscape like a high high sound; loud and clear to those who can and want to hear.

Legends and traditions intermingle. A 'Register of Deaths' in Lamplugh Parish – from Janry ye i, 1658, to Janye ye i, 1663 – includes:

Frightened to death by fairies	3
Bewitched	4
Old women drowned upon a trial for witchcraft	3
Led into a horse pond by a will o'the wisp	1

Is it a legend or do we take it as part of history, or of the traditional beliefs in that remoter locality? Similarly the stories behind the symbols on the coats of arms of the old families of Cumbria hover between the two. The first Lords of Millom, for example, bore the Horn and the Hatteral – a scalp. The horn can be attributed to the fact that the family were hereditary foresters and the horn was the usual badge of a forester. The scalp however takes us straight into Romance with a young lord being captured and strung up by his hair and his true love cutting him down and rather inexpertly severing the skin of his scalp in the process.

And the 'Lucks' stand in a similar case: the famous 'Luck' of Edenhall, for example, belonging to the Musgrave family. This 'Luck' piece was a glass vase enamelled in red, blue, green, white and gilt. It is thought to have been made in Aleppo in the thirteenth century and brought back from the Crusades – or it was found by a butler of the Musgraves who went to the well for water and surprised

126

The Luck of Edenhall, a glass vase enamelled in red, blue, green, white and gilt, thought to have been made in Aleppo in the thirteenth century and brought to England from the Crusades.

a company of fairies dancing around the goblet which he stole. And they warned him:

> If that glass should break or fall
> Farewell the Luck of Edenhall.

Many people still believe that the precious vase was indeed broken and that this accounts for the demolition of the hall and the extinction of the branch of the Musgrave family. In fact, the 'Luck' is now one of the treasures of the Victoria and Albert Museum; London gets most of the looted luck, as usual.

There's the Luck of Muncaster Castle, the Luck of Burell Green, the Luck of Workington – and all of them intertwine legend, tradition and history most engagingly.

Just as 'Lucks' are everywhere to be found so are the traditions and superstitions about nature and the calendar. Here are a few examples from each of these fertile sources. They take us straight back to the omnipresent gods and goddesses of the Greeks.

To certain trees have always been ascribed supernatural powers.

127

With rowan tree well fenced about
We're safe from every evil.

A sprig of rowan, it is recorded as late as 1897, was sometimes placed with the cream in the churn 'to make it come'. The yew tree had a different property. It was claimed that in it you could see the spirit as it passed from the body at the moment of death. Oak trees were often incorporated into Christian funerals. The hazel provides the richest lore; the forked hazel twig is the most potent in water divining, and burials with hazel wands and leaves have been found all over Cumbria. All this is recorded in detail in Marjorie Rowling's excellent *Folklore of the Lake District*. She writes that it is still believed in Cumbria that the bringing of May blossom into a house will be followed by death or news of a death. And she goes on to detail particular trees in the district which have associations and rhymes about the weather (rain, invariably) and birds –

> If crows be on the fallow,
> You'll be dry tomorrow,
> If crows be on the leas,
> You'll be wet to your knees.

Rhymes figure prominently in what is called Calendar Lore. Candlemas Day (2nd February) is cluttered up with them. Rain again.

> If Cannelmas day be fine and clear,
> We'll hev twa winters in ya'eer,
> If Cannelmas day be sunny an' warm,
> You may mend yet auld mittens and luck fer a storm.

Before that of course is New Year's Eve and Day which still goes strong, if my own regular experience in Cumberland is a useful guide. There's First Footing, the dark-haired man, the lump of coal, the penny and the bread. And the alien Scottish fire water which fits snugly into the old lore.

April or May still bring out the Fools and Goslings before the clock strikes twelve noon; and the church festivals in the 'fifties, certainly, I remember for their association with pussy willow, carlins, hot cross buns and Pasche eggs almost as much as for their Church-based Christianity. The Pasche eggs were particularly vivid. Throughout the town people would compete to decorate those very hard-boiled eggs. Some of them were gorgeous, streaked with

In the eighteenth and early nineteenth centuries it was common to hold public weddings to which there were open invitations – but the 'guests' were expected to finance the proceedings with gifts of money.

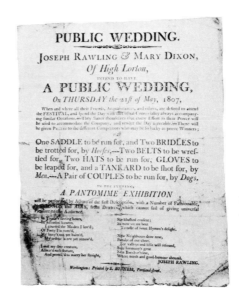

colours from different dyes. The second competition was to bash them against each other, like conkers, to find the champion egg. Before my time the eggs were rolled down a hill which was known as Pasche Egg Hill. And so it goes on through to 5th November and Christmas. The same pattern reveals itself; as in other outlying districts of the United Kingdom, local traditions here are held more intensely and have probably lasted longer.

It is not easy to be sure in any claims for local peculiarity. Many traditions are shared – either with other parts of the 'Celtic Fringe' – especially Ireland; or with other parts of the north – especially the West Riding of Yorkshire. When Harriet Martineau, for example, reports of the refusal of mothers to wash their children, in Wasdale, she brings in the similar condition of Yorkshire. Talk of folk dress – hardy, home-made stuff – and folk medicine – sometimes alarming, sometimes sensible – can scarcely be localized either. Yet it might be useful to list two or three of the everyday customs prevalent until quite recently.

There were the Bidden Weddings and the Bidden Funerals. The weddings were like public dances; the entire valley would be invited along and not only food and drink, but sports and prizes for sports would be laid on all day. There was 'throwing the stocking', a raunchy bedding custom which is perhaps the precursor of the decorous throwing of a bouquet.

Death brought out the usual harvest of superstitions; no one, it was believed,

129

It was widely held that if a corpse was carried over privately owned land, the route would become a right-of-way. This document, dated 28th March 1687, concerns Joseph Sunton who took the body of his mother-in-law from Claife near Hawkshead to Grasmere Church over several of his neighbours' fields. Here he states that '. . . I doo believe that I had noe right to goe that way but by permission or asking leave. . . .'

could die on a bed containing pigeon feathers. As soon as a person died it was necessary to 'tell the bees' and often the hive would be decorated with a black ribbon. Guests could be 'Bidden' to a funeral as well as a wedding – the difference sometimes lying in the fact that the guests would contribute a small sum to defray the expenses of the bereaved. And in days when graveyards were not omnipresent, there were ritual 'corpse ways' along which the body was drawn. Arval cake was eaten at the funeral. The number of times the bell tolled indicated the nature of the deceased; the Troutbeck 'passing bell' tolled nine times for a man; six times for a woman; three for a child.

A tradition which still exists – at Warcop, Musgrave, Ambleside, Grasmere and Urswick – is rush bearing. The women of the village collect together with clean rushes and go to the church in procession.

To end this, though, in the proper past, I would like to quote a quiet piece which shows the detail and community of Cumbria only a hundred and fifty, even a hundred years ago. This piece also has the merit of introducing to the book one of the few dishes for which the area is peculiarly and rightly famous – rum butter. It was written by John Briggs about a hundred years ago.

Rum Butter for a Lying-in.
Previous to the time [i.e. of the birth], a quantity of sweet butter was prepared; for many of the Dale-landers believed that a lying-in woman would never recover unless

130

A nineteenth-century rush bearing outside St Oswald's Church, Grasmere.

she had plenty of sweet butter. It was thus prepared. The butter was melted (not boiled) in a brass pan, till the milk ran to the top, and the salt sunk to the bottom. The milk was then scummed off, and the butter decanted clear from the salt. A quantity of rum and sugar, having been well beat together in a bowl, with a little grated nutmeg, was then mixed with the butter, when all was stirred till the mixture began to cool. Thus prepared, it would keep for any length of time; and few houses were without a pot of sweet butter at all seasons of the year. On this occasion, or at funerals, a certain range of families was called 'the laiting'; the principal females of which were laited (sought out). So soon as the child was born, its head was washed over with rum . . . Before the women departed, they sat down to tea, whatever time of day or night it might be. As soon as the good woman could bear to sit up, the neighbouring women were invited to a second tea party, called the "wiving", when they all attended with presents – some brought bread, butter, sugar, wine or any thing deemed necessary at such a time. A great deal of etiquette was observed on these occasions. It was a great insult if one within the laiting was forgot in the general

131

Rush bearing at Grasmere. Once a necessary act to replace the old rushes on the church floor, the rushbearing ceremony has become a children's flower festival.

invitation. It was also an insult, if one of them was not invited till after the child was born.

John Briggs, Canon Rawnsley, John Richardson, Dorothy Wordsworth – these are just a few of the writers who have raked the legends and superstitions of the area. Although such customs as 'rum and butter for lying-in' are now observed only nominally and in the remoter districts, there is still that pulse of continuity in trace memories, patterned on the past like faded landmarks on an old map.

Opening up

1

For the last two hundred years, the Lake District has absorbed wave upon wave of those looking for physical, sensual, psychological and spiritual refreshment. They have come to look at the valleys, climb the rocks, saunter by the waters, contemplate the hills; and sometimes they have stayed to build and breed. The most amazing feature of all is that despite the incessant influx, the place is still rich in the qualities sought here: serenity, danger, splendour and variety of experience. 'Canny ol' Cumbria' indeed.

Camden's *Britannia* (1644) marks a useful starting point. Of Cumberland he wrote:

> Although it be somewhat with the coldest, as lying farre North, and seemeth by reason of hilles, yet for the variety thereof it smileth upon the beholders, and giveth contentment to as many as travaile it. For, after the rockes bunching out, the mountains standing thick together, rich of mettal mines, and betweene them great meeres stored with all kinds of wild fouls, you come to pretty hills for good pasturage and well replenished with flocks of sheep, beneath which again you meet with goodly plaines spreading out a great way, yeelding corne sufficiently.

In 1671 Sir Daniel Fleming wrote about the county, though more on his ancestry than the place itself. The first truly independent visitor was the Honourable Celia Fiennes who boldly rode around England side-saddle and interested herself in everything she saw. Writing in an endearingly gossipy and jolly way of the Ups and Downs of Travel, she came to Windermere:

> Thence I rode almost all the waye in sight of this great water [i.e. Windermere]: sometymes I lost it by reason of the great hills interposeing and so I continu'd up hill

Daniel Defoe, after van der Gucht.

and down hill and that pretty steep even when I was in that they called bottoms, which are very rich good grounds, and so I gained by degrees from lower to higher hills which I allwayes went up and down before I came to another hill; at last I attained to the side of one of these hills or fells of rocks which I passed on the side much about the middle; for looking down to the bottom it was at least a mile all full of those lesser hills and inclosures, so looking upward I was as farre from the top which was all rocks and something more barren tho' there was some trees and woods growing in the rocks and hanging over all down the brow of some of the hills.

On a more commercial venture – the first (excluding Camden who was, after all, doing a public service) of many who have turned an honest penny by describing the district – the great Daniel Defoe set out to tour the whole Island of Great Britain and had these rather dampening and sensationalist remarks to make.

This part of the country seemed very strange to us, after coming out of so rich, populous and fruitful a place, as I have just now described [i.e. Preston]; from here we were, as it were, locked in between the hills on one side high as the clouds, and prodigiously higher, and the sea on the other, and the sea it self seemed desolate and

134

Scafell and the Sty Head track, one of the most important pack-horse routes through the fells.

wild, for it was a sea without ships, here being no sea port or place of trade, especially for merchants; so that, except colliers passing between Ireland and Whitehaven with coals, the people told us they should not see a ship under sail for many weeks together.

Here, among the mountains, our curiosity was frequently moved to enquire what high hill this was, or that. Indeed, they were in my thoughts, monstrous high; but in a country all mountainous and full of innumerable high hills, it was not easy for a traveller to judge which was highest.

Nor were these hills high and formidable only, but they had a kind of unhospitable terror in them. Here were no rich pleasant valleys between them, as among the Alps; no lead mines and veins of rich ore, as in the Peak, no coal pits, as in the hills about Hallifax, much less gold, as in the Andes, but all barren and wild, of no use or advantage either to man or beast. Indeed here was formerly, as far back as Queen Elizabeth, some copper mines, and they wrought them to good advantage; they are all given over long since, and this part of the country yields little or nothing at all . . .

Here we entered Westmoreland, a county eminent only for being the wildest, most

135

Part of Christopher Saxton's map of Cumberland and Westmorland, 1576.

barren and frightful of any that I have passed over in England, or even in Wales it self; the west side, which borders on Cumberland, is indeed bounded by a chain of almost unpassable mountains, which, in the language of the country, are called Fells, and these are called Fourness Fells, from the famous promontory bearing that name, and an abbey built also in ancient times, and called Fourness.

'Barren and Frightful' it remained for a long time. On some sleety days there are those of us who would not flinch before the adjectives now. In the mid-eighteenth century, the civilization of the outer regions of Britain gathered pace; the failure of Bonnie Prince Charlie's rebellion produced a feeling of safety, turnpikes were opened, roads were improved, highwaymen pursued, inns enlarged, travel made easier, maps developed, and the exploration of the native islands got under way.

Christopher Saxton's Map (1576) served as the basic guide for the explorers for many years and, looking at it now, its priorities mirror the needs of the times. The rivers were well marked and so were the bridges; the hills need not have existed. The aim clearly was to move on safely and avoid danger. In the next century the pen of the artistic cartographer brushed ever more intensively on the page – Speed in 1610, Blaeu – nominated as the peak of the art – in 1645, and Ogilby in 1675 – but all of them were based on Saxton and all were more like picture books than present-day maps. The hills were still little blobs daubed in carelessly in the knowledge that no one wanted to know much about them.

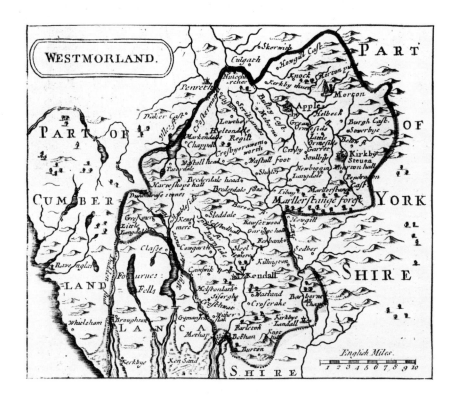

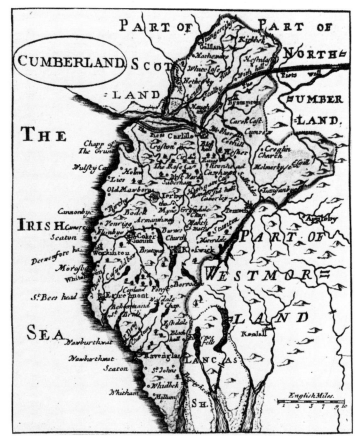

Two eighteenth-century maps of Cumberland and Westmorland. Both are very inaccurate and are largely based on the much earlier work of Christopher Saxton and John Speed.

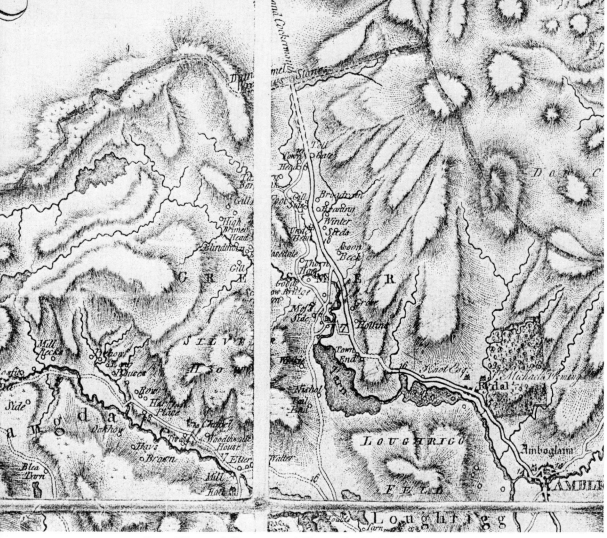

Part of Thomas Jeffery's map of Westmorland, 1770; scale: one
inch to a mile. Although there are no contours or spot heights,
an attempt has been made to show relief by hachures.

In the second half of the eighteenth century, many more maps were rushed
out to meet the gathering fashion – Bowles, Carrington, Kitchen and Bowen
were among the map-makers – but the hills were still not well marked and when
the Lakes appeared they were often little more than hopeful puddles of ink put
in as much for the picture as the accuracy. But, as usual, prosperity demanded
more information and as the roads, particularly in Westmorland, improved, so
did the maps. In 1770, stimulated by the Society of Arts, Thomas Jefferys

138

'Morning Amongst the Coniston Fells'. J. M. W. Turner.

'Storm over Derwentwater – Evening'. John Constable.

'Castle Crag, Borrowdale', *c.* 1812. J. C. Ibbetson.

'Grasmere by the Road'. Francis Towne.

The Slate Quarry Wharf, Clappersgate, 1805. J. Harden.

The Bridge House,
Ambleside, 1946. Kurt
Schwitters.

'Cumbrian Landscape' by Sheila Fell.

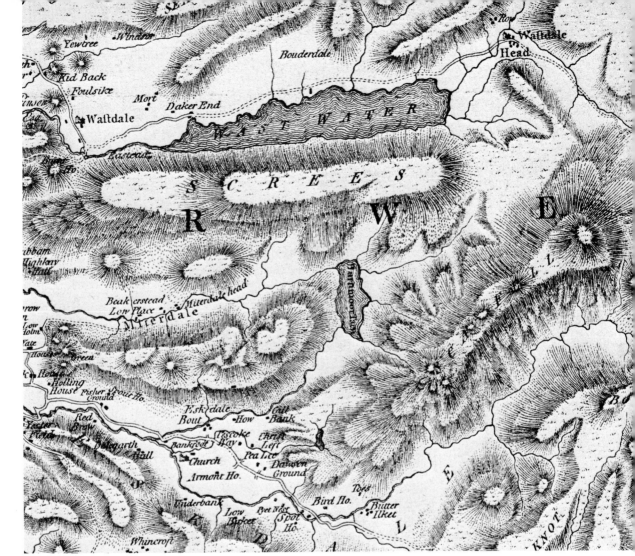

Part of Joseph Hodgskinson and Thomas Donald's map of
Cumberland, 1774. This was drawn – as reproduced here – to a
scale of one inch to a mile and was the first truly accurate map
of the county.

produced his excellent maps of Westmorland and a few years later, Hodgskinson and Donald brought out at last a recognizably accurate Cumberland. Most
of the roads were shown; farms and hills were named; the coastline pointed in
the right direction and wriggled more or less as it should have done: the Lakes,
though, were still puddles. Finally, of course, came the magnificent Ordnance
Survey in 1860 and all was revealed.

Entrance into Borrowdale: after J. Smith.

It is pleasing for me to record that the first man to make a publicly recorded poetic statement about the Lake District was a Wigtonian. In 1751, Dr John Brown, a local vicar who had practised the trade of playwright in London and the role of clergyman in Penrith, wrote this in the *Gentleman's Magazine*. He was speaking of the view from Skiddaw. 'The craggy precipices' (of neighbouring mountains) 'have the appearance of large fragments of rock irregularly heaped on one another but in the prospect round: nature has lavished such variety of beauty as can scarce be believed upon report, or imagined by the most luxurient fancy.' Four years later, Dr Dalton, another local man – from Dean near Cockermouth – reported on the beauties of the Borrowdale area in verse.

But it was Dr John Brown's *Description of the Lake and Vale of Keswick*, printed at Newcastle in 1767, which alerted Arthur Young and Thomas Gray to the possible riches of the Lakes and could be said to have been vital in starting the new fashion. It is satisfying to local pride that home-grown men set off what began and still is a great pilgrimage to the Lake District. But it was Thomas Gray who made the great impact on the new travelling public with his description of a short visit in 1769.

It was the new fashion. Scenery – A Natural Place. The combination of scientific enquiry and the conquest of a home-grown wilderness. The Town, swarming with life and art, with commerce, conversations and wit, with money, men, buildings and fashion, the Town, which should have satisfied Dr Johnson's man, was moving out for fresher pleasures. Beyond the city, uncivilized England called and Gray, a fragile scholar, author of the most famous elegy in the language, responded. He set off on a ten days' tour of Cumberland. He took his 'claude-glass' with him – a little mirror in which the landscape could be framed. The most famous passage in the influential work (most widely read as an appendix to Thomas West's *Guide to the Lakes*) which came out of the tour, was this account of his visit to Borrowdale.

Oct 3 [1769] A heavenly day; rose at seven, and walked out under the conduct of my landlord to Borrowdale; the grass was covered with a hoar-frost, which soon melted and exhaled in a thin bluish smoke; crossed the meadows, obliquely catching a diversity of views among the hills, over the lakes and islands, and changing prospect at every ten paces . . . Our path here tends to the left, and the ground gently rising, and covered with a glade of scattered trees and bushes on the very margin of the water, opens both ways the most delicious view that my eyes ever beheld. Opposite, are the thick woods of Lord Egremont, and Newland valley, with green and smiling fields embosomed in the dark cliffs; to the left, the jaws of Borrowdale, with the turbulent chaos of mountain behind mountain, rolled in confusion; beneath you and stretching far away to the right, the shining purity of the lake reflecting rocks, woods, fields, and inverted tops of hills, just ruffled by the breeze, enough to shew it is alive, with the white buildings of Keswick, Crosthwaite church and Skiddaw for a background at a distance. Behind you the magnificent heights of Wallowcrag; here the glass played its part divinely . . .This scene continues to Barrowgate, and a little farther, passing a brook called Barrowbeck, we entered Borrowdale, the crags named Lowdore-banks begin now to impend terribly over the way, and more terribly when you hear that three years since an immense mass of rock tumbled at once from the brow, barred all access to the dale (for this is the only road) till they could work their way through it. Luckily no one was passing by at the time of this fall; but down the side of the mountain, and far into the lake, lie dispersed the huge fragments of this ruin, in all shapes and in all directions: something farther we turned aside into a coppice, ascending a little in front of Lowdore water-fall; the height appeared to be about 200 feet, the quantity of water not great, though (these three days excepted) it had rained daily in the hills for near two months before; but then the stream was nobly broken, leaping from rock to rock, and foaming with fury. On one side a towering crag, that spired up to equal, if not overtop the neighbouring

The Bowder Stone, Borrowdale.

cliffs (this lay all in shade and darkness); on the other hand a rounder, broader, projecting hill, shagged with wood, and illuminated by the sun, which glanced sideways on the upper part of the cataract. The force of the water wearing a deep channel in the ground, hurries away to join the lake. We descended again, and passed the stream over a rude bridge. Soon after we came under Gowdar-crag, a hill more formidable to the eye and to the apprehension, than that of Lowdore; the rocks at top deep-cloven perpendicularly by the rains, hanging loose and nodding forwards, seen just starting from their base in shivers. The whole way down, and the road on both sides is strewed with piles of the fragments, strangely thrown across each other, and of a dreadful bulk; the place reminds me of those passes in the Alps, where the guides tell you to move with speed, and say nothing, less the agitation of the air should loosen the snows above, and bring down a mass that would overwhelm a caravan. I took thus counsel here, and hastened on in silence.

Gray teased some of the London literati into thought and action. The coaches filled up. The fashion was set rolling. The Lake District became the New World for the Metropolis.

146

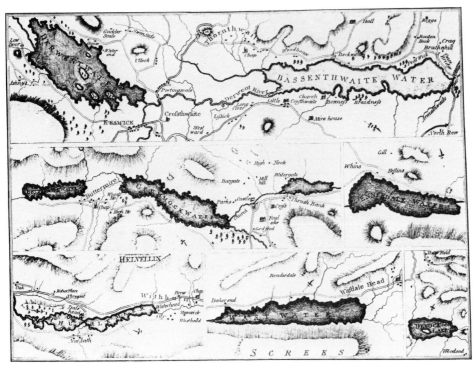

The Lakes in Cumberland from Hutchinson's *History and Antiquities of Cumberland*, 1794.

In 1773–4 William Hutchinson came on his *Excursion to the Lakes*. He described not only the place, but the legends, such as the Phantoms of Souther Fell, and the carnival effects which could now be seen and heard in a district which quickly became enterprising in the embellishment of its charms. Cannons were let loose on Ullswater and the visitors carefully recorded the echoes in the mountains. The wilderness could be turned into a playground and the edge of danger preserved as a distant thrill. The early visitors wanted to enjoy feeling dominant and enjoy a sense of the primitive at the same time: the Lake District suited them well.

More space is demanded for William Gilpin who made his journey a year before Hutchinson. In one sense it was a journey back home. Born of a genteel and literary Cumbrian family, he went south, made a success in the profession of schoolmaster and began his quasi-scientific investigations into landscape. He too made great use of the plano-convex mirror – the 'claude'-glass. He justified this: 'where the objects are great or near it removes them to a distance and shows

147

Historical and artistic licence – Honister Crag showing a battle
in progress between kilted Highlanders and mounted troops.

them in the soft colours of nature and in the most regular perspective the eye can perceive or voice demonstrate'. Nature in the raw was still best left as a prospect – not to be tackled face on.

Gilpin's approach is easy to parody, but its carefulness is in some way admirable. Here he is trying to educate his readers: his subject is the mountains of this region.

> With regard to mountains, it may be first premised that, in a picturesque view, we consider them only as distant objects; their enormous size disqualifying them for objects at hand. In the removed part of a picture therefore, the mountain properly appears; where its immensity, reduced by distance, can be taken in by the eye; and its monstrous features, losing their deformity, assume a softness which naturally belong not to them.

Paragraph follows paragraph as he explains how the hills can be tamed, reorganized, framed and made acceptable to what he saw as the best standards of taste.

Gilpin wrote the right book at the right time. Its immense popularity propelled scores of the more adventurous and sensitive of a leisured upper middle class out of the cities and out of the urbane country houses hot-foot for 'being melancholy among the ruins'.

148

Scale Force, the highest of all the Lakeland waterfalls, was the object of considerable nineteenth-century admiration.

Brown, Gilpin, Wordsworth: it is tempting to see this trio of Cumbria-born men – all of whom, incidentally, went out of their county, south, at crucial times in their careers and returned to solder the reappraisal of a convert to the understanding of a native – as being that direct succession whose laying on of words opened the eyes of the multitudes and brought them into the pastures of Lakeland. Not quite so. We have already mentioned Thomas Gray: now we must acknowledge Thomas West, whose *Guide to the Lakes*, published in 1778, was enormously influential in opening up the twin counties.

West, as scientific in his way as Gilpin, brought in the notion of 'stations', that is, particular viewpoints where the 'best' view could be obtained. These 'stations' provided a detailed grand guide for many years to come and they still reward attention. Here is West – a Catholic priest, an antiquarian of note – describing Coniston in terms of the best 'station'.

> Station 1. A little above the village of Nibthwaite, the lake opens in full view. From the rock, on the left of the road, you have a general prospect of the lake, upwards. This station is found by observing where you have a hanging rock over the road, on the east, and an ash-tree on the west side of the road. On the opposite shore, to the left, and close by the water's edge, are some stripes of meadow and green ground, cut into small inclosures, with some dark coloured houses under aged yew trees. Two promontories project a great way into the lake; the broadest is finely terminated by steep rocks, and crowned with wood; and both are insulated when the lake is high. Upwards, over a fine sheet of water, the lake is again intersected by a far-projecting promontory, that swells into two eminences, and betwixt them the lake is again caught, with some white houses at the feet of the mountains. And more to the right, over another headland, you catch a fourth view of the lake, twisting to the north-east . . .

And the stations are plotted out all about the lake. The fashion swelled.

Soon, Jane Austen's Miss Bennet was looking forward to her visit to the Lakes. The satirical Dr Syntax had beaten her to it – but his lampooning of Gilpin only added to the fashion. Gentle satire is a form of gentle flattery. Peter Crosthwaite made his detailed maps of the Lakes and was appointed Admiral of Mr Pocklington's 'Fleet' on Derwent Water. Regattas were organized; grandiose houses built; a Tom Thumb version of Castlerigg's stone circle was constructed on Derwent Isle. The place had become an amiable retreat for the rich, who wanted nature without blood, toil, tears or sweat. There was some percolation down the social scale. Less rich families took marquees for an entire summer; canvas caravans hoisted for the Lakeland voyage.

Pocklington's Island, Derwent Water, 1786.

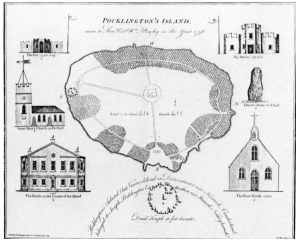

Joseph Pocklington, a rich
eccentric, constructed a series
of follies and pseudo-antiquities
on Derwent Isle in Derwent
Water. Wordsworth thoroughly
disapproved. . . .

The beginnings of commercial
tourism; Peter Crosthwaite, at
one time 'Admiral of the
Keswick Regatta . . . Guide,
Pilot, Geographer and
Hydrographer to the Nobility
and Gentry', kept a museum at
Keswick. 'Admittance to
Ladies and Gentlemen, One
Shilling each; Country People,
Sixpence each . . .'. 1792.

The Round House on Belle Isle, Windermere. According to Wordsworth this was the 'first house that was built in the Lake District for the sake of the beauty of the country . . .' but another writer, William Gell, suggested that it looked 'exactly like a large shop tea canister'.

But it was the vastness of nature and its even vaster possible moral implications which at the turn of the century changed the place from being the spa of the rich into the mecca for all sorts of pilgrims of the spirit. The man who brought this about was Wordsworth. His poetry is discussed later. Two points are worth making here. Firstly, his notion that the grandeur of nature was both in itself remarkable and even more remarkable for the moral balm and correction it could administer to the properly prepared soul. This idea soon struck deeply into the minds of a thoughtful middle class conditioned to be religious but less and less nourished by Christianity. Secondly, Wordsworth preached the simple life – always alluring to those who do not have to lead it day in and day out. Wordsworth led it. And he believed in it. Again, it made you better. 'In the condition of life' (in rural modesty) 'our elementary feelings co-exist in a state of greater simplicity . . . the manners of rural life germinate from those elementary feelings . . . in that condition, the pains of men are incorporated with the beautiful and permanent form of nature.' The awe, the moral philosophy and the humanity of Wordsworth ensured that from then on the Lakes would be no passing show: a place had been found where complicated and profound satisfactions and solace could be sought and found.

Taste and *Rural Simplicity* on the shores of Windermere with the Round House on Belle Isle much in evidence. From Plaw's *Rural Architecture*, 1794.

2

The settlers began to arrive in force. Some of them built grand houses – one of the first was put up on Belle Isle on Windermere by the aptly named Mr English of Nottingham. Alas for the luck of the English, the local worthies took against it and he sold up pre-completion to Miss Curwen whose subdued version was approved. Soon the house became a proud local landmark.

The southern Windermere area drew most of the new building. This was the period when many of the bigger houses in the area were constructed or extended and the turn of the century – 1800 – or a few years later saw the establishment or substantial enlargement of such notable piles as Armathwaite Hall, Rydal Old Hall, Coniston Hall, Hutton Tower and Low Wood Inn. The new houses came complete with new theories and Richard Payne Knight even put them into verse. The growth in number of these mansions and the development of landscape gardening provided one of the biggest changes in the landscape at that time. People used to tour about the place just house – and celebrity-spotting – as if dour Cumbria were a precursor of Beverley Hills.

These 'off-comers' – as new settlers were and still are called – were as often in

Left: Professor John Wilson ('Christopher North') – the scholar-athlete who claimed to have bathed in every stream and lake, climbed, walked, and wrestled with the local 'heavies'. *Right:* Harriet Martineau. Her mid-nineteenth-century guide book cast a critical eye on the locals.

pursuit of health as beauty. Their champion was Professor John Wilson, as 'Christopher North', the scourge of the *Edinburgh Review*. It was the physical vigour of the man, though, which ensured the passage of his reputation around the Lakeland. He claimed to have bathed in every stream and lake, he climbed, he wrestled with the local heavies: add this to his literary activities and friendships and you have the hearty-arty prototype or, more politely, the scholar-athlete, who was to become so much more common towards the end of the century.

By the 1820s, the generality were arriving at Windermere teased in by all the writers. As contemporary prints and engravings show, the place swarmed with toffed-up industrial gentry on a spree. A whole new Lakeland town, Windermere, grew up to accommodate the visitors, and Grasmere, Keswick and Ambleside too began to turn to tourism. The Lakes were the principal draw. The hills, for most visitors, were to be peered at from a carriage or looked up to

Built by a Liverpool surgeon, Dr James Dawson, between 1840–47, Wray Castle is a huge pseudo-Gothic pantomime set-piece which dominates the western shores of Windermere.

from an easy slope. Ruins, grand houses and, as the mid century drew on, the Wordsworths, were the other favourite sights. And in 1840 there was a royal visit. The Lake District had passed through fashion and was welcomed with the royalty of respectability.

The railways arrived in the 1840s and another stratum of society steamed up to the North-West.

The railways brought prosperity to the new towns like Windermere, a touch of splendour to a spot such as Grange over Sands, and a series of failed resorts along the coastline from Seascale to Silloth. Harriet Martineau's brisk new guide of 1855 provided the ideal handbook for the new tourists – and she recommended the mountains although she cautioned her readers that local shepherds were necessary for the bigger fells. She had a very unromantic eye for the locals and seemed to delight in pointing out their dirtiness and backwardness. One particular passage is chilling.

The Priory Hotel, Windermere. A mock-Gothic turreted fantasy which exhibits all the confidence of the *nouveaux riches* settlers of the post-railway age.

Haweswater reservoir from above Riggindale.

The linen and woollen webs woven by [the peasant] his wife and daughters would not sell, except at a loss, in the presence of the Yorkshire and Lancashire woollens and cottons made by machinery. He became unable to keep his children at home, leaving home yet more cheerless, with . . . more temptation to drink. Having reached this pass, it is clearly best the process should go on till the primitive population, having lost its safety of isolation and independence, and kept its ignorance and grossness, shall have given place to a new set of inhabitants.

That this did not happen must be due in some part to the general increase in wealth which came from the tourist boom.

The second half of the nineteenth century is best seen as a clever containing action. John Ruskin, who was intoxicated by the place from the age of five when he stood on Friar's Crag and eventually bought Brantwood in Coniston, fought hard against the railways (as did Wordsworth). He wrote of the 'lower orders', 'I

157

John Ruskin by George
Richmond.

do not wish them to see Helvellyn while they are drunk.' A reservoir for an
industrial town struck him as yet another example of that industrial avarice
which was corrupting mankind and he fought hard against the extension of
Thirlmere.

In those battles he was aided by many of the local worthies – often newly
settled – keen to keep the place as they had found it. Outstanding among them
was the indefatigable Canon Rawnsley whose 30,000 sonnets and support of
innumerable causes (including raising the tone of comic postcards and re-
introducing maypole dancing) made him a valuable – voluble ally. Yet despite a
most memorable fight, with the prose and the arguments reaching a notably
high standard, the level of Thirlmere *was* raised and the lake *was* lengthened,
considerably. At the official opening in 1892 none other than the ubiquitous
Canon proposed the toast. Just as surely, the railways came bringing, not the

Yewtree Farm and 'spinning gallery' near Coniston. These galleries were used not only for spinning of yarn but also for other processes associated with the woollen industry.

Gathering Swaledale sheep in Kentmere. The fourteenth-century pele tower, built against Scottish incursions, is a reminder of more troubled times.

Castlerigg Stone Circle. John Keats is known to have visited the circle and perhaps this prompted him to write in *Hyperion* of gods

'. . . like a dismal cirque
of Druid stones, upon a forlorn moor,
When the chill rain begins at shut of eve,
In dull November, and their chancel vault,
The heaven itself, is blinded throughout night.'

The inheritors of a long tradition – dry-stone wallers at work.

William Wordsworth. B. R. Haydon.

The most famous huntsman of all – John Peel. By all accounts he was 'terrible land in t'leg and lish (agile) with a girt neb (nose) and grey eyes that could see for ivver'. Clearly this portrait is fanciful.
From an oil painting by J. H. Smith.

Beatrix Potter. D. Banner.

The steam railway in the second half of the nineteenth century brought not only a new method of transport but new settlers and a new way of life.

industrial vandals feared by the Wordsworthians and Ruskinites but, on the
whole, sober and earnest citizens principally from Lancashire who took the
place to their hearts and became, in turn, jealous of its amenities.

It was they who came willingly into the National Trust, founded by Rawnsley
and others in 1895. If you cannot beat them, Rawnsley's motto seems to have
been, get them to join you.

Few would question the efficacious results of the founding of the Trust.
Today it is far and away the biggest landowner in Lakeland and its thoughtful
policies – though not without mistakes and critics – have managed to conserve
while not being exclusive. The quickest way to illustrate that is to say that
although more than three million visitors a year now come into the Lakes, it has
emerged over the last years as Europe's leading breeding ground for those easily
disturbed birds, eagles and peregrine falcons. Between these two extremes, the

Man versus Nature: the reservoir and plantations at Thirlmere
and the western slopes of Helvellyn.

Brockhole, the Lake District National Park's visitors centre on the shores of Windermere.

Trust walks what seems to be a practised tightrope – widely supported by volunteer help and by what appears (touch wood) to be a tradition of reasonable attentiveness to the needs of the landscape.

Roads have now been widened and motorways built. You can cruise up from London in four or five hours, you can zip by the Lakes on broad fast routes. Hotels, camping and caravan sites, hostels and second homes have made it accessible to all sorts of people – Tynesiders in Keswick for their fortnightly holiday, hard men from the Midlands up on the rocks, Southerners looking into Dove Cottage and foreigners 'doing the Lake Poets'. There's now a centre – Brockhole – which inwardly reflects the wealth of the area. Its exhibitions, slide shows and excellent historical and naturalistic displays, now bring in almost 200,000 people a year. The museums have prospered – particularly the excel-

Ullswater and Place Fell.

Fishermen on the shore of Coniston Water.

lent Abbot Hall in Kendal and the new Wordsworth Museum at Grasmere. There are yachting clubs, pony trekking centres, bird watching sanctuaries, rivers and lakes to fish, hills to hunt. Yet, despite all the charabancs and wireless warnings of floods of tourists which occur around each Bank Holiday, any regular visitor or any local resident will tell you, truthfully, that even at the height of the season, you can be virtually on your own among the hills in a matter of minutes. It is a spectacular example of a place being at once undeniably popular and indisputably a refuge. And it is the almost infinite interfolding of hill and valley which most gives it that double life.

There are drawbacks: complaints of villages 'dead' out of season because those with second homes flit back to the city; complaints that local people are being driven out because of the high price of property; complaints that the broad routes to the familiar peaks are now so trodden that they have become an eyesore. Truth in all this – but no one can grudge the pleasure given now to so many by this place: and if a balance were to be drawn up, surely the benefits to

Skiers on Raise above Glenridding.

Many Lakeland footpaths, like this one in Great Langdale, are
threatened with over-use.

Samuel Taylor Coleridge by
Peter Vandyke.

the district itself – apart from that enjoyed by those who come and go – would
outweigh the disadvantages. The place is now open to all sorts and conditions of
men, women and children and so far humankind has treated this rare inheritance quite well.

3

Rock-climbing deserves a section on its own and it makes a fitting conclusion to
this chapter. For out of the central feature – the rock – came a sport, a tradition
and stories which not only enriched the twin counties but helped substantially
to give the world a new dimension in adventure and physical daring. These
climbs soar above the valleys of amblers and the slopes of school-party walkers
to find a new wilderness on the bare rocks.

It is impossible not to introduce this section by way of Samuel Taylor
Coleridge whose famous accidental descent of the south side of Scafell

169

prompted him to write what is generally regarded as the first record of a rock climb – or rather, a descent. The date is 1802.

Eskdale, Friday, Augt 6th at an Estate House called Toes (Taw House). A Ridge of Hill lay low down, and divided this Crag (called Doe-Crag) and Broad-Crag – even as the hyphen divides the words broad and crag, I determined to go thither; the first place I came to, that was not direct Rock, I slipped down, and went on for a while with tolerable ease – but now I came (it was midway down) to a smooth perpendicular Rock about 7 feet high – this was nothing – I put my hands on the Ledge, and dropped down. In a few yards came just such another, I dropped that too. And yet another, seemed not higher – I would not stand for a trifle, so I dropped that too – but the stretching of the muscle of my hands and arms, and the jolt of the Fall on my Feet, put my whole Limbs in a Tremble, and I paused, and looking down, saw that I had little else to encounter but a succession of these little Precipices – it was in truth a Path that in a very hard Rain is, no doubt, the channel of a most splendid Waterfall. So I began to suspect that I ought not to go on; but then unfortunately tho I could with ease drop down a smooth Rock of 7 feet high, I could not climb it, so go on I must, and on I went. The next 3 drops were not half a Foot, at least not a foot, more than my own height, but every Drop increased the Palsy of my Limbs. I shook all over, Heaven knows without the least influence of Fear. And now I had only two more to drop down – to return was impossible – but of these two the first was tremendous, it was twice my own height, and the Ledge at the bottom was exceedingly narrow, that if I drop down upon it I must of necessity have fallen backwards and of course killed myself. My limbs were all in a tremble. I lay upon my Back to rest myself, and was beginning according to my custom to laugh at myself for a Madman, when the sight of the Crags above me on each side, and the impetuous Clouds just over them, posting so luridly and so rapidly to northward, overawed me. I lay in a state of almost prophetic Trance and Delight and blessed God aloud for the powers of Reason and the Will, which remaining no Danger can overpower us!

His faith and boldness – and luck – got him down to live to write and climb another day.

Half a century later, Alpine mountaineering began, pioneered by Britishers. The second half of the nineteenth century was the time when many sports were given their present-day profiles – the rules, the clubs and the institutional status: tennis, croquet, football, rugby, boxing, sailing – in that great flourish of Victorian organizing confidence, there was time and energy to colonize everything, including leisure. Rock-climbing benefited from the movement

The eastern face of Scafell. Broad Stand lies to the left of the ridge in the centre of the picture; Coleridge's descent of this rock face in 1802 marks the beginning of English rock climbing.

although, from the beginning, it was something of an outsider, perhaps too individualistic for the group sense of the age. The Alpine Club, for example, not only looked down on the Lakeland rock-climbers socially, they put a very low value on the activity itself despite the fact that, faced by the rocks of Cumbria, their members rarely performed well. Rock-climbing brought out that personal questing which was and is at the heart of many people's reasons for journeying to the Lakes.

The coastal railway was completed in 1857, linking to the main line at Carnforth; and the link between Ravenglass and Eskdale (1875) enabled rock-climbers to come within hearty walking distance of what became the centre of the new sport – Wasdale Head.

Alan Hankinson, in his book *The First Tigers* is understandably intoxicated with the 'type' of man who came to Wasdale Head at the beginning of the 1880s.

171

The Keswick Brothers – Ashley and
George Abraham, photographers
extraordinary.

Perry Haskett Smith would seem typical – reading Plato in the mornings,
exploring new routes in cracks and gullies in the afternoon. Hankinson sums
them up.

They were highly educated men, the products of public school and university,
steeled in the discipline of science and mathematics, the classics and the law. They
approached their climbing in an academic spirit. They admired courage and skill and
style. The thing they despised most of all was boastfulness. They recommended
climbs to one another because they were "interesting" or "presented a pretty little
problem". They would debate for hours about the relative merits of certain routes,
the ideal patterning of nails in their boots, whether repeated ascents made a climb
more easy or more difficult. They took a lively interest in the geology of the crags, the
wild life of the fells, the agriculture of the dales, the history of the Lake District and
the derivations and meanings of its placenames. Their conversation, as they fought
their way up difficult pitches, was often more evocative of a Senior Common Room
than of a rock climb. Classicists and Senior Wranglers were much in evidence. Latin

172

Napes Needle: The solo ascent of this pinnacle by Haskett Smith in 1886 has been described as 'the most significant short climb ever accomplished'.

tags sprang naturally to their lips, and when Haskett Smith narrowly avoided death on one of his early climbs he found himself, by his own account, clinging to a ledge and muttering an appropriate line from Homer in the original Greek. "Climbing then," said Geoffrey Winthrop Young, "had the freshness of a dawn!"

This lyrical assessment is backed up by our knowledge of such men as Professor Collie, O. G. Jones, the Hopkinson, Pilkington and Walker brothers besides such more occasional participants as Quiller-Couch, Alastair Crawley and Leopold Amery. To guide these off-comers, though, were local men. After all, sixty years before all the intellectual 'outsider' Wasdale Head excitement about the ascent of Pillar Rock, it had been climbed by John Atkinson of nearby Ennerdale. Some of the best climbing teams were a combination of local and visitor: Haskett Smith of Cambridge and J. W. Robinson of Lorton; O. G. Jones of London and the Abraham Brothers of Keswick. The rock-climbing photographs taken by the Abraham Brothers are not only spectacular in them-

173

Owen Glynne Jones – the first of 'the hard men'.

selves, but they too might be said to have set in train a new movement in photographs – the studied search for the spectacular. They went on to take photographs in other mountainous regions of Europe and their postcards have become collectors' items.

What happened in those few years was the opening up not only of the rocks and the climbs but of a new and very taxing sport. In 1886, Haskett Smith climbed Napes Needle alone and this, according to Hankinson, was 'the most significant short climb ever accomplished and some see it as the true beginning of the sport'.

Today there are 50,000 rock-climbers in Britain, and the Fell and Rock Climbing Club publishes eight guide books to the climbs in the Lakes, listing and describing in ever more detail the thousands of routes up scores of cliff faces. It is hard to realize how uncharted those comparatively small surfaces of rock then were. Half of the genius of that group was to identify a challenge; the other half was to rise to it.

O. G. Jones has been described as the first of the 'hard men'. An immensely muscular climber, idolized by the Abraham brothers, thought by others – especially Crawley – to be too reckless, he stands out as the epitome of all the zest and conquest of the time. His death in the Alps when he was merely thirty-two gave a tragic shape to his life. His commitment up on the rocks of Cumbria cannot be read without a feeling of affection for the drive of the man. Here is his description of his climb up Walker's Gully.

The precipice was a grand study in black and white, its immense slabs shiny black with a thin veneer of ice, and decorated artistically with snow festoons and long slender icicle tassels. Verily the giant had donned his coat of mail, and meant to do his best to repel our attack; but his preparations were incomplete. A little more ice on the middle obstacle, a little further loosening of a splinter of rock at the top pitch, and we should have been driven back unsuccessful. Maybe he thought us too wise to attempt the climb under such adverse conditions; but we were not, and the mistake spelt his defeat.

We roped at the foot of the crags, and I started up by the left of the gully. The direct route could have been taken with greater ease, but a solid jet of ice-cold water was jetting straight down the middle, and we preferred to keep dry a while longer. I mounted the wall from ledge to ledge, turning periodically at distances of four or five yards to manipulate the rope for the second man, who in his turn steadies the last man up. It is easier, not to say far more pleasurable, to climb than to describe the process.

Keeping up the wall for 60 feet, we were then able to traverse along a narrow terrace into the gully, and the hard work began in earnest. Vertically upwards sprang the great cleft, with massive boulders many tons in weight dividing it into separate storeys like the rungs of a gigantic ladder. On our heads dripped the water thawing from the upper rocks, uncomfortable at first, but preferable to the vagrant falling stones that haunt the locality in the summer time. There was no drift of snow that might help us up the first few feet of each pitch. The side walls were clothed in wet ice. We wriggled up yard by yard, working closer together now for mutual aid. So long as the gully remained narrow, we were safe, for it was easy to hold in by leaning across from side to side.

Then came the first overhanging bit at the middle pitch, and while Field braced firmly in the innermost recesses, steadying my rope, the second man balanced himself astride the gully, outstanding on the slenderest of ledges. Then I clambered on to his shoulders to reach the outer edge of the roofing-stone that overhung our course. Its upper surface was steeply sloping, and a jet of water pumping on to its centre radiated out a spray of icy liquid from which there was no escape. Sharp was the word, for strength and courage languish rapidly under such penetrating influences. But I could find nothing to hang on to, so smoothly lubricated did every hold seem, until an aperture was discovered in the roof through which a loop of rope could be passed from below. This served excellently, and I hastily drew myself up with its aid. The others followed with greater speed though they could not dodge the waterfall, and we stayed a moment to wring out our coats before continuing the assault.

If variety were charming, we had charmed lives. Up the next ladder we went, through one obstacle, over the next and "chimneying" up between the third and the great wall, the leader using the shoulders and heads of his companions, their upstretched hands steadying his precarious footholds, and their expert advice supporting him all through. And with it all the most sublime views outwards and upwards and downwards of Nature's simple and severe architecture, designed and executed in her grandest style.

At last we came to the final obstacle, the limit of previous exploration. We had arrived at a little platform deep in the mountain, and three enormous boulders, one on top of the other overhanging more and more near the top, had to be circumvented. There was no way behind them; the only possibility was to work up one side wall and climb past them. I flung off my boots and Norfolk jacket, expecting to give the second man a bad time standing on his shoulders at the take-off, and attempted to climb up a narrow fissure in the left wall. Unhappily it proved to be useless, and we were all supremely uncomfortable when it was discovered that I should have to descend again.

Next the right wall was tried and I blessed the previous three months' monotonous training with heavy dumb-bells. The strain on the arms was excessive. Fortunately, there was no running water there, or the cold would have been unendurable. At the worst corner, by hanging on with the right hand, and with the left looping part of my rope through the recess at the side of the boulder, a good grip was improvised. Of natural holds there were none on that smooth, icy wall and the loop was a perfect boon. Even a perfect boon is hard to utilize when hands and toes are benumbed and all one's muscles are racked with prolonged tension. But the loop served its purpose and after a few more struggles in the crack a ledge was reached from which it was evidently an easy scramble to the head of the gully.

"*Reussi – parfaitement – messieurs –* send up my coat and boots". The gasping message was finished in English to save delay, but I shiveringly waited many minutes in soft snow before the rope could be untied and the articles in question slung up on it. A cherished pair of socks fell out of the coat pocket as it was hauled over the edge of the top boulder, and took a preliminary clear drop of two or three hundred feet. It gave us quite a shock at the time, for we thought it was a packet of sandwiches.

Then my companions came up, with an enviable surplus of warmth and energy. We raced up the steep snow and rock that remained above us, and did not halt till we had crossed the fell and descended to our starting point near the foot of the Pillar Rock. There we sat in a protected corner, and I put my frozen feet into others' pockets, my dignity into my own, while we ate the crushed remnants of our lunch and discussed the day's excitements. When the grateful diffusion of animal heat had brought sensation to my extremities and the spare energy of the whole party had spent itself in dragging on my boots, we started off again and made our way over the snow-covered fells down Wastdale.

Today, from this base in the Northern Fells, Chris Bonnington organizes expeditions to India, South America and China. The mountain ranges of the world are increasingly available for assaults in which British climbers still figure prominently. But the clink of climbing gear and the steady instructions of young men apparently glued to a flat rock-face, still sound richly about the Lakes. First the valleys, then the villages, then the lakes, the lower slopes, the fells; and finally the rock was found and that too yielded totally unexpected benefits as, over the last two hundred years, the Lake District has been opened up to a public who find in it so many varieties of delight, consolation and adventure.

A Victorian climb – a snow gully on Great Gable.

9

The Painters

This ought to be a chapter for looking at as much as for reading. Over the last two hundred years, so many paintings and engravings have been made of this district that the mass makes the mind falter. I have several hundred photographs and reproductions in front of me as I write and the attempt to put a pattern on them has yielded several possibilities. There is the good old chronological route – a pathway I have trodden regularly in this book until it is as wide and worn as the road to the top of Skiddaw! Another method would be to use the occasion to attempt to show the change in the appreciation of the countryside – from the melodramatic views of Thomas Smith in 1761 to the dramatic views of Sheila Fell in 1961; and between the two everything from the cosy to the coy with the strong theme of 'realism' or verisimilitude working its way through steadily. It is also possible to think of starting with photographs of some of the most popular views and comparing several different paintings to the photographs to compare approximateness to that particular 'truth'. And should we stick to Cumbrian painters or to those who have painted Cumbria?

In 1980 there was a most enterprising exhibition laid on at Abbot Hall in Kendal. The idea was to take nine of the most popular 'scenes' in the Lakes, show the geographical aspect of the view and then bring together as many paintings, etchings and engravings as possible to illustrate how variedly this view had been interpreted. It worked marvellously well. But the overwhelming impression given by the exhibition was the pleasure which came from seeing so many paintings. Stepping inside the gallery, and being met by such a display, there was no doubt what you wanted to do: follow your eye, go to the paintings which most attracted you, make up your own patterns.

So in this chapter I intend to treat the painting and painters of the district as if

'Falls of Lodore' by J. M. W. Turner.

they were all in a gallery. To browse around the estate. The historical line is intertwined with the opening up of the place described in the development of tourism and poetry. In the second half of the eighteenth century, engravers came to aid and service the embryonic popularity of the Lakes: the trickle became a flood so that by the turn of the century there were literally hundreds of studies being sold in London. In the nineteenth century the interest continued and spread into all the tributaries of Victorian painting and although there has been some slackening off in the present century, some superb photographs have kept up the representations of the district.

Turner did the greatest paintings of the Lakes. 'Morning Amongst the Coniston Fells' and his dark study of Scafell stand as supreme among all other paintings as Wordsworth's poetry stands among other poets. The Coniston painting more emphatically registers the look and atmosphere than anything else I have seen. By contrasting the brooding, dark, boggy foreground with the

179

rain-cleared, airy, almost other-worldly background Turner immediately captures the most common and pleasing characteristic of this place: that you can be in the middle of several sorts of weather at the same time. But that is just the beginning of it. The textures of the water, the clouds, the distant Langdales, the heavy, sodden ground, the washed translucent sky are all so powerfully depicted that the sense of recognition, for me, is instantaneous. 'Morning Amongst the Coniston Fells' transmits the feeling of a place not only in its particular sense but also in the most general terms: this vibrant but desolate spot could illustrate that day in Genesis when God made the waters – and the force of its naturalness obliges us to realize that this will still be there when homo sapiens has run his race.

More prosaically, though, what we see in Turner, just a few decades after the area had been discovered, was that he penetrated it to the heart. He brushed aside all the hesitations and embellishments of previous artists: gone the distorted tufted little trees, the picturesquely well-shaped view, the metropolitan idea of a wilderness, the tasteful placing of cattle and gentlefolk as if in an Italian landscape, the fawning inclusion of a great house. Turner came and saw the landscape with a terrible directness and painted it as it had never been painted before and has never been painted since.

Another work, 'Torrent in Spate, Coniston', again shows his genius for getting to the heart of it: here is the landscape at its simplest and most elemental. This is how it is, how it was, how it will be. Turner, in the few works he did in this district, proves the perfect complement to Wordsworth – the poet going into the landscape for values, for intimations of morality, the painter looking at it as a pagan, seeing its power and presence as sufficient cause for wonder.

The Lakes were lucky. Constable came too. Though he did not leave as substantial a legacy as Turner, there is enough for us to enjoy the sight of a great master casting his eye on the place, particularly Derwent Water and Borrowdale. 'Morning – Borrowdale' is entirely divorced from the 'horrid' and excessive images of fifty years of exaggeration and presents the sweep of fells, the gentle curve of the river, the few trees in that undemonstrative way which immediately convinces us that this is how it was. There is not the force of Turner, not that power to make us see afresh and consider not only the beauty of the work but the nature of the place itself, but we see Borrowdale plain. More of his art is in 'Storm over Derwentwater – Evening' where, in a work done with evident speed, he brings off that effect so characteristic of the place – the interaction of sky, fells and water. The heavy-bellied dark clouds darken the fells which run

'The Cascade, Rydal' by John
Constable.

into Derwent Water almost without a break. Yet again, though – as with Turner
on the Coniston Fells – Constable has captured the diversity of the skies: for
though part of it is brooding and darkly dominating, there is an area of clear sky,
in the far distance, which lights up parts of the water, contradicting the
darkness. The other work of Constable which again shows his graphic directness, is a drawing of the 'Falls of Lodore', once again in Borrowdale.

Not only Turner and Constable, but Wright of Derby also passed through the
Lakes and stayed to paint subjects. As with them, there can be no claims that
this area substantially altered his art. Wright of Derby, though, executed the
most serene painting ever done in the place. If Turner found in it the basic
landscape, even the basic elements which were to preoccupy him increasingly,
and Constable used it to further his study of the exact representation of light and
its effects on clouds, earth and water, Wright of Derby's 'Ullswater' presents
that calm study of a lake surrounded by fells which is the peaceful and for many

'Langdale Pikes' by John Constable.

the most satisfying aspect of any walk. There is nothing savage about it – the landscape, though populated only by one man in a boat, is accessible, human, unmenacing. Once again the fundamental contrast has been caught – the sky is light, the hills dark, the centre of the lake shining with light, the edges darkening. The weight of the fells is not oppressive, their size is not dramatized; the whole landscape has an immovable and settled look without being at all cosy.

These three, in my opinion, are outstanding in their depiction of the Lakes. Others who passed through, such as Gainsborough and more extensively Edward Lear whose drawings often capture the more placid face of the landscape, Ivon Hitchens and David Jones whose single works certainly enrich the store, left nothing as weighty and definite as Turner, Constable and Wright of Derby who came, saw and penetrated the heart of it.

Ruskin's work – my favourite is of Thirlmere which he did much to defend against the Manchester Corporation – cannot be said to have added greatly to the pictorial riches of the place: his writings about art, and especially his championing of Turner, were of incomparably greater importance. Coniston

'Thirlmere' by Edward Lear.

'Thirlmere' by John Ruskin.

'Bridge House' by William Green.

provided the setting for them just as Friar's Crag had provided the child Ruskin with the original inspiration for his love of landscape.

A more interesting example of someone who came and stayed and painted here is that of Kurt Schwitters who arrived in Ambleside just before the outbreak of the Second World War and painted local scenes to pay his way, while what he considered his more important work was carried on almost, in his day, unheeded. Yet even in such a painting as 'Bridge House, Ambleside' (he did a great number of these to supply a steady and still unabated demand for a representation of that architectural curiosity), the modernist bite of the man's vision is there to be seen. Where most painters (W. Green, for example) had seen it as a pretty little oddity, a tiny house perched toy-like on a tiny bridge over a small stream, Schwitters, by taking a low angle 'shot', emphasizing the height and its isolation, partly screening it with a tree barely struggling into blossom, gives it a wideness and even a grandeur which is far away from the domesticated quaintness of depictions before and since.

There are a number of Cumbrian-born or Cumbrian-trained artists whose work relates only slightly to the area, but to pass them by would be to do an injustice to the place. The finest of these is George Romney, undoubtedly the greatest Cumbrian painter. He was born (1734) at Beckside in the village of Dalton-in-Furness then in Lancashire. But his training and his base was in Kendal which in the mid-eighteenth century nurtured a school of painters. Most of them were portrait artists, many of them leaving the town to go south, often to London, to improve their art and to make their reputation. But all of them could be said to belong to the 'Kendal school'. Like so many local painters of that time, Romney was the son of an artisan – in his case a joiner and cabinet maker – and found himself nudged and pushed by small acts of patronage until he came under the wing of a comparatively successful artist – in his case the flamboyant scoundrel Christopher 'the Count' Steele. Perhaps George Romney could best be represented here by the portrait of his brother, Peter, who lived under the shadow of George and, after a life disrupted by debts and drink, died unfairly unappreciated.

Next in importance, a century earlier (1615–90?), is Richard 'the Dwarf' Gibson, who was 3 feet 10 inches and by one of those felicities of fate became an eminent painter of miniatures. Taken up by Sir Peter Lely and the court of Charles II, he was nimble enough to swop horses and go to Holland when Princess Mary married William of Orange, to return with them when they came to the throne after the quiet revolution of 1688.

William Gilpin (1733–1807), born in Carlisle into a family of painters, became the most important animal painter – especially of horses – of his day, to be overtaken only by Stubbs. Robert Salomon (or 'Salmon' as he later called himself: 1775–1844) was born in Whitehaven and became a painter of scenes at Whitehaven, Merseyside and Greenock and elsewhere before going to America, where he did his finest work: Americans regard him as an outstanding marine painter. Other Cumbrian-born painters who achieved national reputations outside the area, and whose work largely ignores the place which bred them, include Daniel Gardner (1750–1805), again a Kendal man, several of whose portraits have been attributed to Constable; T. H. Carrick (1802–74) of Carlisle, a very successful Victorian miniaturist; and Robert Smirke (1751–1845) of Wigton, who enjoyed a considerable reputation in his day as a painter of historical scenes.

Before we come to that mass of artists who came to depict the Lakes – some on lightning trips, some to stay for a few years, others to live out their adult lives here, there are four local painters who well deserve mention. William Jones Blacklock (1816–58), though born in London, was brought back to his father's

'Borrowdale' by Sam Bough.

birthplace, Cumwhitton near Carlisle, when he was four. His output was not prolific; his great promise – recognized by Turner among others – never had the time to mature, but such landscapes as we have show a very clearsighted unromantic artist whose sense of the sculpture of the Fells (see 'Catbells and Cawsey Pike') and the weight of the rock gave his work strength and simplicity.

Sam Bough (1822–78) is better known than Blacklock. He was far more prolific and is probably the most affectionately regarded of local painters who depicted the district. Born in Carlisle, the son of a shoemaker, he was trained locally, made his first mark with local scenes, met Wordsworth and his circle and went to Manchester and finally to Scotland, where he decided to become a full-time landscape painter and where he lived for most of his adult life. He was loyal to Cumbria, however, often painting Carlisle (usually from a distance) and returning regularly to the Lakeland landscape. The work is lush, placid and gentle, with neither threat nor much weight to it – but sufficiently well done to be more than merely pleasing. He was interested in the activities of the people almost as much as the landscape itself – this alone distinguishes him – and from the two paintings of Borrowdale, for example, we get a sense, perhaps illusory, of the slow, calm country ways of the time. More famous in his own day than in ours, Bough, whether painting a cricket match, a hayfield, baggage wagons or a lake village, brings something of the flavour of the people – albeit a genteel selection – to his canvases.

Sheila Fell (1932–80) is arguably the most potent of the native Cumbrian painters. Born in Aspatria, she trained in Carlisle and London and with remarkably few exceptions, her landscapes dwell on the area at the edge of the fells. Her work is almost expressionist in the intensity of feeling expressed by the hills and skies, almost always heavy, brooding, threatening. It is a Cumbria full of menace, somewhere between a child's nightmare and the pessimistic vision of a clear and sorrowful mind. Landscape painting of the representational sort which she pursued was so unfashionable in her day that there is an element of wilfulness, of forcing matters in the work. That, too, though, now seems to give it even more power: it was as if the landscape, having dominated her growing mind, had to dominate her painting despite all the good advice she could give herself to the contrary.

The fourth local painter is James Bateman, born in Kendal in 1893, died 1959. His very neat, photographic realism is far from the painting of Sheila Fell and to many it might indeed seem too modelled and tidy. Nevertheless there is undoubted authenticity and critics have praised the skills of the man, and for many, the very photographic appearance which seems to me rather bloodless, gives Bateman's work both distinction and value.

Bateman's precise, almost dry, depictions of the landscape seem more than two hundred years away from that flurry of engravers who rushed up to the Lakes as it struck popularity in order to cash in on the mini-boom. Kenneth Smith, in his *Early Prints of the Lake District*, draws attention to many of these jobbing engravers and he starts with his namesake Thomas Smith ('of Derby'). He went all over England drawing, engraving and publishing, and his views of certain lakes published in 1761 most aptly show the pre-Wordsworthian attitude to nature. 'A view of Windermere' for example makes it look like a failed volcanic lake. The mountains sweep upwards like quiffs from the shore; the clouds spiral to the heavens like belching smoke; someone rather like a matador drives something rather like mules in the foreground and the lake ripples one way while the trees sway another. The detail and gusto cannot be

'View of Windermere' by Thomas Smith of Derby (1761).

denied; the verisimilitude is marginal; and the thrill of horror intended is quite harmless – there is a frail bark comfortably perched mid-lake which assures all potential visitors that they will be safe and sound in this little Italy of the North. His 'View of Derwentwater' is even more amazing and amusing: Borrowdale disappears entirely under a spread of cloud while the hills rise up with all the force of inky sponges.

Perhaps it is too easy to mock; but it proves irresistible again and again with those early engravers. William Bellers, for example, who worked the district a little earlier than Smith, produced, among others, 'A View of Derwent-Water From Vicar's Island Towards Skiddaw'. Once again the detail, indeed the clutter, is impressive but there is no settled notion of landscape or indeed of place. The title tells us where we are, but little in the frame encourages us to really believe it. Carefully and fashionably dressed people decorate the fore-ground, appetizers for the metropolitan purchasers, while the lake, the hills and the sky are as gay as those of Smith are grim: Come, says T. Smith, and be

Thomas Smith's 'View of Derwentwater' (1767).

thrilled with safe horror: Come, says Bellers, and be soothed with somnambulistic sweetness.

The Reverend William Gilpin (1724–1804), born at Scaleby Castle near Carlisle, was probably the most effective of the popularizers. His books and theories on picturesque beauty, his advocacy of the claude-glass, and his rhapsodies on ruins appealed directly to the new public bent on discovering in England what they were barred by the French wars from seeing abroad.

Christian Rosenbery was yet another who came to praise, and between 1784 and 1789 Joseph Farrington published twenty plates of views. There is a placidity about Farrington which is not unappealing and though he lacks the edge of Sam Bough – many of whose paintings were transformed into engravings – there is a more than ordinary journeyman honesty about these prints which make them a decent record. Another Smith, John 'Warwick' (1749–1831), is even more Italianate than his namesake Thomas but, like Bough, his inclusion of local activity – for example the 'Ferry on Windermere'

Skiddaw and Derwent Water depicted by W. Bellers, 1774.

which shows horses being ferried across the lake in shallow-bottomed row-boats, gives an added social interest.

There were many others, including Thomas Dibdin, whose view of Ambleside shows that town in an extraordinarily calm, enviably pretty light; William Westall, who, again, introduced local incident but drained the fells of all feeling; John Laporte; Thomas Allom whose mistiness produces such a hazy impression that all definition is lost; Wheatly; Rathbone and the Reverend Joseph Wilkinson whose forty-eight views published in 1810 were the occasion for Wordsworth's introduction which twelve years later became his *Description of the Scenery of the Lakes in the North of England* and later still, his famous *Guide to the Lakes*. Rowlandson, in his Dr Syntax series, satirized these engravers, Gilpin especially, to great effect.

William Green (1760–1823), who settled at Ambleside in 1800, is typical of the movement. He produced an enormous number of paintings and engravings, became a friend of Wordsworth and his circle and found sufficient employment and pay in the district to live well by popularizing it through his many works.

'The Eagle Crag in Borrowdale' by C. Rosenberg after P. Holland.

Though not of high quality, Green, like the others, shows the force of that fashion which was turning attention to the countryside and demanding representations and reminders.

Colour printing gave a boost to the industry, and the finest is that in the 1853 edition of J. B. Pyne's *The English Lake District*. In 1880, J. Walker produced a book of coloured prints and again the results are excellent.

These engravings, which poured out regularly from 1750–1850, were easily displaced by the arrival of photography. The Abraham brothers; the Mayson family; there were many local enthusiasts and experts whose talents were often

'Dr Syntax Sketching the Waterfall at Ambleside' – one of Rowlandson's unpublished drawings for Dr Syntax's 'Tour'.

'Ullswater' by William Green.

at first directed towards making photographs look like engravings. Moreover, they were framed, named and cherished in such a way as to make it clear that they were thought of as objects of value and record – every bit the equal of the engravers. The engravers, though, the etchers and hacks, who bolted up north, swallowed the place down in one or two bites and then pounded back to their presses, have left us with an account both of the slowly changing landscape and the almost equally slowly changing attitude of the middle classes – who were both the producers and consumers of these works. It is easy to smile at them, and impossible, often, not to find them a little dull. But it is important to remember that, in the first flush, certainly in the eighteenth century, they were doing something new, opening up a hinterland of England for the enlighten-ment of those who never knew it existed and drawing attention to the countryside as a subject of value to be compared with portraits, historical paintings and society groups.

As the Victorian age unrolled, a curious phenomenon occurred in Cumbria and perhaps elsewhere. Almost as an apparently unconscious response to the Victorian call on the virtues of Family, families began to settle in the area and their several members would all paint. There were the Heaton Coopers whose most gentle but accurate paintings and watercolours show a Lake District emptied of all horror, most of its grandeurs and all of its danger – a pleasant docile spot. To be fair, Alfred Heaton Cooper (1863–1929) did bring a feeling of contemporary Cumbria – especially to some of his townscapes – which are a definite addition to the store of work on the area. Yet his Cumbria would not stir or harm a careless babe – and for some people this is the place they find.

There are the Tuckers, at least five of them, four of them the sons of Edward (1825–1909); and all of them, including one who became the Bishop of Uganda, painted industriously, chiefly in watercolour; and here too we have a placid, quietly happy Lake District – more like a backwater than a frontier – which was indeed the general trend as the century went on. There had already been the Gilpins in the previous century; now there were the Nutters, the Carlyles of Carlisle and the Collingwoods, father, W.G.; his wife; and two daughters. W. G. Collingwood, who worked alongside Ruskin for many years, was a careful scholar of the area – in watercolour, history, geology and antiquity.

Charm, though, had triumphed by the end of the century and its apothesis can be found in the tiny landscapes hidden behind those timeless creations of Beatrix Potter, who freely and precisely acknowledged her connection with the district. Arthur Ransome, whose books on children drew deeply from his own

'The Painter's Home' by Julius Caesar Ibbetson.

childhood in the Lakes, turned to illustration in despair at finding anyone who could see his creations as he himself saw them – and those, too, show the charm the place had for the comfortable, largely cheerful, well-off people who settled down in the district and domesticated it as they domesticated the length and breadth of their own lives.

In a brief survey such as this, the sight of the end draws out the cries of outrage at the omissions. No Joseph Simpson (1879–1939), whose illustrations decorated hundreds of Cumbrian walls for years? No William James Linton (1812–98), wood-engraver extraordinary? No Newcombe, no Samuel Crosthwaite with his excellent portrait of Dorothy Wordsworth? Nor Girton, nor Sir George Beaumont much admired by Wordsworth? The list could be enormous. I would like to conclude with two men who were here at the height of Cumbria's artistic fame and who, in different ways, left a fine representation of the place.

Julius Caesar Ibbetson (1759–1817) came to Rydal Water in 1798 and stayed in the district for five years. His often massive paintings have the excitement of

194

'Ambleside, The Market Place' by Julius Caesar Ibbetson.

discovery coupled with the professionalism of an artist who feels that he has found a subject at once fresh and commercial. 'Ullswater from Gowbarrow', and 'Castle Crag, Borrowdale', have a majesty and certainty which shows off the district – cattle, children and kindly well-dressed groups included – to flattering advantage; and yet we feel that the man had something grand and personal in his response to these scenes. Wordsworth is more in him than in the much more direct Turner or the more tentative and almost scientific Constable. And in his 'Ambleside, The Market Place', there is an attempt to portray the community, which is so rare in the Lakes painters that we are grateful for it.

More than grateful, then, for the work of John Harden of Brathay Hall (1772–1847). He lived for thirty years at the head of Windermere and never exhibited in his lifetime despite the encouragement of admirers such as John Constable. What has been discovered since his death, and made the subject of a book by Daphne Foskett, has been an enormous number of interiors. Odd to end indoors when the greatest work has depicted the world outside. But these watercolours, sketches, oils and drawings of middle-class life show us the hidden factor in most of the paintings over the last two hundred years; the patrons, the appreciators and the customers. Here they are, at their pianos, in their drawing rooms, reading, playing cards, singing, sewing, painting, posing, 'Waiting for the Irish Packet', 'Dozing the Thimble', observing a Dame School, a Quill Winder, the milking, the market, the laundry, until, in 1843, the whole delightful series comes to a perfect end with a portrait of John Harden himself – a photograph.

'On Windermere' by John Harden.

The Writers

Wordsworth now seems so inevitably and inextricably bound up with Cumbria that it is a jolt to realize the haphazard, almost casual way in which he came to spend the greater part of his adult life there. He arrived at Dove Cottage, when he was in his late twenties, partly out of a sentimental curiosity but – much more importantly – in search of cheap lodgings. The lodgings, true, had to be situated in or near nature – but the much milder Quantocks and other parts of Southern England had provided all the background and foreground Wordsworth needed for the *Lyrical Ballads*.

It is tempting to believe that, though he may have arrived in Grasmere accidentally, he remained because the recognition of home and childhood came so strongly on him that he was ensnared. The facts, though, show that his own beloved boyhood was already working in his imagination and had surfaced in the poetry well before he returned to his home county. Moreover, in the first five or six years following his return, he was often prepared to up and go: in which case what is now the great chapter in Cumbrian life would have been no more than an episode. But he stayed. For his last fifty-two years he lived in one house or another within a few miles of where he and Dorothy had landed in 1799. And in that time the link between the place and the man did become inextricable and moved out of the sphere of chance and into the area of total inevitability.

There are those who refuse to believe in accidents and indeed there were powerful unconscious forces which, it could be claimed, were drawing him inexorably back to the fells. He was born there, in the handsome market town of Cockermouth; his fertile life at the Grammar School in the large village of Hawkshead provided memories – mostly happy – for a lifetime; the natural features which had helped form him were largely unchanged on his return and seemed, for some time, unchanging.

Yet there were reasons as powerful for him never wanting to see the place again – a great deal of pain, humiliation, embarrassment, the jagged edge of failure which causes many a recoil. It was not so much the particularity of the place which either drew him or held him – much as he came to use the place's special features. It was nature, which, to him, was 'all in all'.

> The moving accident is not my trade:
> To freeze the blood I have no ready arts
> 'Tis my delight alone in summer shade,
> To pipe a simple song to thinking hearts.

By the grace of fortune, then, he came back to his roots and there grew into what his friend Coleridge claimed as our third poet after Shakespeare and Milton – a judgement still widely accepted today. Ted Hughes, for example, one of the finest living poets, has said that 'when you look back, Wordsworth is the first mountain-range you see'.

There were a few who had written poetry describing the local landscape before Wordsworth. Dr John Brown, from Wigton, had written verses which, we know, Wordsworth read and appreciated. Another local versifier was Dr Dalton. He begins his description of the beauties of the Vale of Keswick in true pre-Wordsworthian terms – more than forty years before Wordsworth's Lakeland poetry.

> Horrors like these at first alarm,
> But soon with savage grandeur charm,
> And raise to noblest thoughts the mind.

Despite a distinct falling away from noble thoughts in the rest of the verse, the appreciation of nature on this particular plane was already under way.

And besides the local poets, as we have seen, there were a number of travel writers, including Gilpin, Budworth, West and Hutchinson – and, perhaps most influential, the poet Gray – most of them from outside the district – who had opened the place up to a larger public and begun to describe it in resonant lines. Wordsworth immortalized it.

He was born in 1770 in Cockermouth, second son of John, an attorney at law. John was an agent for Sir James Lowther. It was a job which often took him away from home. The house they lived in was and remains a very handsome town house fronting the main street, well protected from the ordinary towns-folk – backing on to the River Derwent which was later remembered by the poet with great pleasure.

> Oh! Many a time have I, a five years child,
> A naked boy, in one delightful rill,
> A little mill-race severed from his stream,
> Made one long bathing of a summer's day,
> Basked in the sun, and plunged, and bask'd again.

There were four brothers and Dorothy. William, even in what proved to be a brief and steady (if not happy) stretch of normal domestic life, was thought, by his mother, to be 'stiff, moody and violent'. She told a friend that he would be 'remarkable either for good or evil'.

He was eight when his mother died. He mentions her very little. She must have been suffering the exhausting cycle of child bearing for much of his childhood: her illnesses and his moods would seem to have kept them apart – or did they mark him for life? Too little is known of her. After her death the family was split up and Dorothy was sent south to Halifax – he did not see her again for nine years. William spent most of his time at the notable Hawkshead Grammar School, lodging with Ann Tyson who appears to have been a most easy, comfortable and yet financially careful landlady and mother-hen. When he was thirteen his father died, leaving him not only an orphan, but unprovided for. His father's earnings had been held back over the years by the wealthy Low-thers and now they refused to honour their debts. From then on, William was to be constantly beholden to others for the slightest expense, and the experience directed him to a frugality – wholly admirable – and a shrewdness – often less laudable – which was to stamp his character for life.

Holidays – grim affairs by the sound of it – were passed again locally, in Penrith. It was Hawkshead, however – then an affluent little town – which was the centre of his universe and can be seen as a true root of his genius. He was fortunate in Ann Tyson; fortunate again in the brilliant young headmaster William Taylor who urged him to read and write poetry and, as he saw it, twice blessed in the place itself.

> Fair seed-time had my soul and I grew up
> Fostered alike by beauty and by fear;

199

Much favoured in my birth place, and no less
In that beloved Vale to which, ere long,
I was transplanted.

In *The Prelude* – mostly written in Cumbria but begun before he returned – he describes 'the growth of a poet's mind' in wonderful detail. There you can find the weight of his affection for his schooldays – the climbing, poaching, skating, nesting, kiting, riding, boating. There too, something of the 'fear' he refers to.

In his childhood Wordsworth was subject, as recorded by his mother, to violent tempers and rages even against himself, and even up to the point of trying to kill himself. In early manhood he endured awful depressions; even in his famous and well-shod middle age he was often struck down by what seem to have been psychosomatic symptoms. If he knew the harmonies which came from a contemplation of beauty he also knew the disorders and disconnections which came from that inexplicable 'natural' fear which often induces violence. There is enough evidence to suggest that at certain times in his life, he was threatened by a serious breakdown. At least once when that happened as a boy, he clutched on to the rocks literally to hold to the world. The chasm closed. Nature saved his sanity. His powerfully sensitive awareness of the moods of nature could not have been so profound had he not understood the fear as much as the beauty; and the fear led him to look on nature as a healer. That duality, more than anything, characterizes the relationship the poet Wordsworth had with nature. And he came to see it as a source of moral strength; a potential influence on character.

> One impulse from a vernal wood
> Can teach you more of man
> Of moral evil and of Good
> Than all the sages can.

Nature is the teacher.

> She has a world of ready wealth
> Our mind and hearts to bless –
> Spontaneous wisdom breathed by health
> Trust breathed by cheerfulness.

His life in Cambridge – again described in *The Prelude* – began well, ended badly. He came out of it unqualified for any profession and unwilling, it seemed, to do anything about it. He walked half-way across Europe, stayed with friends, planned half a dozen aborted enterprises in London and then, back in France, on a haphazard enterprise to prepare for teaching, met Annette Vallon, fell in love with her, made her pregnant and left for England.

He told Dorothy about it and she instantly wrote to Annette, welcoming her as a prospective sister-in-law. He told one or two of his friends – but later, become the Grand Old Man, he was very inclined to forget it when he lectured youth on morality. The war between England and France prevented him getting back to Annette. His prospects were bleak: no money, unfit and unwilling to be a clergyman, not much use at any job he thought of, disinclined to think much beyond the ideal or the hopeless. The war dragged on for ten years without a break and his daughter was born illegitimate; meanwhile William's sanity was saved by Dorothy's attentive love; his prospects were rescued by an inheritance from a young acquaintance who saw William's talent and endowed it with enough barely to live on; and his mind was eventually fertilized by his meeting with Coleridge.

It was undoubtedly a triumvirate of talent out of which his genius grew. Dorothy with the eyes and details, Coleridge with the philosophy and grand ambitions – and William with the slow-burning powers warmed ceaselessly by two of the most complementary helpers any artist can ever have had. For Dorothy's letters and journals reveal a vivacious chronicler whose pages bring alive the time vividly; and Coleridge, then and since, has been seen as not only a fine poet but one of our greatest thinkers on literature.

This happy trio, then, walked, talked and cultivated poetry. Their alliance began well before he returned to Cumbria. Here are the last lines of 'Tintern Abbey' which show not only his ease and confidence, his philosophy and grandness, but also his love for Dorothy.

> Therefore let the moon
> Shine on thee in thy solitary walk;
> And let the misty mountain winds be free
> To blow against thee: and, in after years,
> When these wild ecstasies shall be matured
> Into a sober pleasure, when thy mind
> Shall be a mansion for all lovely forms,
> Thy memory be as a dwelling-place
> For all sweet sounds and harmonies; oh! then,

If solitude, or fear, or pain, or grief,
Should be thy portion, with what healing thoughts
Of tender joy wilt thou remember me,
And these my exhortations! Nor, per-chance –
If I should be where I no more can hear
Thy voice, nor catch from thy wild eyes these gleams
Of past existence – wilt thou then forget
That on the banks of this delightful stream
We stood together; and that I, so long
A worshipper of nature, hither came,
Unwearied in that service; rather say
With warmer love – oh! with far deeper zeal
Of holier love. Nor wilt thou then forget,
That after many wanderings, many years
Of absence, these steep woods and lofty cliffs,
And this green pastoral landscape, were to me,
More dear, both for themselves and for thy sake!

The preface to the *Lyrical Ballads* was also written in the South. This, now regarded as one of the key statements about poetry, contains his famous declaration that he would 'choose incidents and situations from common life – and relate or describe them throughout, as far as possible, in a selection of language really used by men; and at the same time throw over them a certain colouring of the imagination, whereby ordinary things should be presented to the mind in an unusual way . . .' And later: 'All good poetry is the spontaneous overflow of powerful feelings . . . but . . . produced by a man who, being possessed of more than usual organic sensibility, had thought long and deeply etc.' And: 'Poetry takes its origin from emotion recollected in tranquillity: the emotion is contemplated till, by a species of reaction, the tranquillity gradually disappears and an emotion, kindred to that which was before the subject of contemplation, is gradually produced and does itself actually exist in the mind.'

The *Lyrical Ballads*, like most of his early poetry, met with massive in-difference, some viciousness and little praise (and that generally from friends). But he was launched . . . And then he came to Grasmere.

In Dove Cottage, Dorothy managed a very careful household; William just about survived on a friend's bequest and was not too proud to send grovelling letters whenever he could; most importantly, though, the poetry kept coming. The major work of those first years in Grasmere was *The Prelude* which seems to

Honister slate quarries.

St Anthony's Chapel, Cartmel Fell, built about 1504, one of several pre-Reformation chapelries founded to serve the growing population of the Lakeland dales.

Sizergh Castle, south of Kendal. The tower, which can be dated to about 1340, is one of the largest pele towers in Cumbria and was built as a defence against the Scots.

Cockermouth in winter.

Hodge Close slate quarry near Little Langdale. Now abandoned, the former quarry face has become a popular climbing ground.

On the margin of cultivation - Dash Farm on the Skiddaw range near Bassenthwaite villiage.

Overleaf: 'The Sea to the West': sunset at Ravenglass.

me to grow richer every time I read it. The 'Immortality Ode' came from those early years: the first two stanzas show the confidence and care he felt in his work at that time.

I.   There was a time when meadow, grove,
     and stream,
The earth; and every common sight,
    To me did seem
Apparelled in celestial light,
The glory and the freshness of a dream.
It is not now as it hath been of yore:–
   Turn wheresoe'er I may,
     By night or day,
The things which I have seen I now can
   see no more.

II.   The Rainbow comes and goes,
And lovely is the Rose;
The Moon doth with delight
Look round her when the heavens are
   bare;
Waters on a starry night
Are beautiful and fair;
The sunshine is a glorious birth;
But yet I know, where'er I go,
That there hath past away a glory from
   the earth.

There are many poems in which we can see directly the influence of Dorothy – most famously 'Daffodils'. This is her Journal.

Thursday 15th (April 1802). It was a threatening, misty morning, but mild. We set off after dinner from Eusemere. Mrs Clarkson went a short way with us, but turned back. The wind was furious and we thought we must have returned. We first rested in the large boathouse, then under a furze bush opposite Mr Clarkson's. Saw the plough going in the field. The wind seized our breath. The lake was rough. There was a boat by itself floating in the middle of the bay below Water Millock. We rested again in the Water Millock Lane. The hawthorns are black and green, the birches here and there greenish but there is yet more of purple to be seen on the Twigs. We got over into a field to avoid some cows – people working, a few primroses by the roadside – woodsorrel flower, the anemone, scentless violets, strawberries, and that

211

On an excursion along the shores of Ullswater in April, 1802, William and Dorothy
Wordsworth saw the Gowbarrow daffodils. Dorothy recorded the scene in her Journal (below)
and later, clearly influenced by his sister, William wrote his famous poem.

at last under the boughs
the trees, we saw that there
was a long belt of them ~~the~~
~~dreariness near~~ along the
shore, about the breadth
a country turnpike road.
I never saw daffodils so
beautiful they grew among
the mossy stones about & about
them, some rested their heads
upon these stones as on a
pillow for weariness & the
rest tossed & reeled & danced
& seemed as if they verily
laughed with the wind that
blew upon them over the lake, they
looked so gay ever glancing
ever changing. There was
here & there a little knot
& a few stragglers a few
yards higher up but these
were so few as not to disturb

starry yellow flower which Mrs C. calls pile wort [i.e. the lesser celandine]. When we were in the woods beyond Gowbarrow park we saw a few daffodils close to the water-side. We fancied that the lake had floated the seeds ashore and that the colony had so sprung up. But as we went along there were more and yet more and at last under the boughs of the trees, we saw that there was a long belt of them along the shore, about the breadth of a country turnpike road. I never saw daffodils so beautiful, they grew among the mossy stones about and about them, some rested their heads upon these stones as on a pillow for weariness and the rest tossed and reeled and danced and seemed as if they verily laughed with the wind that blew upon them over the lake, they looked so gay ever glancing, ever changing. This wind blew directly over the lake to them. There was here and there a little knot and a few stragglers a few yards higher up but they were so few as not to disturb the simplicity, unity and life of that one busy highway. We rested again and again. The bays were stormy, and we heard the waves at different distances, and in the middle of the water, like the sea.

And his poem.

> I wandered lonely as a cloud
> That floats on high o'er vales and hills,
> When all at once I saw a crowd,
> A host, of golden daffodils;
> Beside the lake, beneath the trees,
> Fluttering and dancing in the breeze.
>
> Continuous as the stars that shine
> And twinkle on the milky way,
> They stretched in never-ending line
> Along the margin of a bay;
> Ten thousand saw I at a glance,
> Tossing their heads in sprightly dance.
>
> The waves beside them danced; but they
> Out-did the sparkling waves in glee;
> A poet could not but be gay,
> In such a jocund company:
> I gazed – and gazed – but little thought
> What wealth the show to me had brought.
>
> For oft, when on my couch I lie
> In vacant or in pensive mood,
> They flash upon that inward eye

Which is the bliss of solitude;
And then my heart with pleasure fills,
And dances with the daffodils.

Wordsworth continued to use the local area for his poems. The rivers, lakes and mountains are named and became a presence; birds and flowers are described both by Dorothy and by William; local incidents, local characters, local battles – all become material for the work which went on until the mid-part of the century. My favourite from the 'Cumbrian' poems is 'Michael', the story of an old shepherd whose son leaves the fells for London, squanders his life and his moral patrimony and dies. 'Michael' is the most moving story Wordsworth told.

Yet the poems which still most often catch my breath are the gentle 'Lucy' poems – inspired by Dorothy? By an unknown first love? By Mary (later his wife)? Or just inspired? These tender mysterious lines show a passionate side of Wordsworth.

Strange fits of passion have I known:
And I will dare to tell,
But in a Lover's ear alone,
What once to me befell.

When she I loved looked every day
Fresh as a rose in June,
I to her cottage bent my way,
Beneath an evening moon.

Upon the moon I fixed my eye,
All over the wide lea;
With quickening pace my horse drew nigh
Those paths so dear to me.

And now we reach the orchard-plot;
And, as we climb the hill,
The sinking moon to Lucy's cot
Came near, and nearer still.

215

What fond and wayward thoughts will slide
Into a lover's head:
'O mercy!' to myself I cried,
'If Lucy should be dead!'

*

She dwelt among the untrodden ways
Beside the springs of Dove,
A maid whom there were none to praise
And very few to love:

A violet by a mossy stone
Half hidden from the eye!
Fair as a star, when only one
Is shining in the sky.

She lived unknown, and few could know
When Lucy ceased to be;
But she is in her grave, and, oh,
The difference to me!

*

A slumber did my spirits seal;
I had no human fears;
She seemed a thing that could not feel
The touch of earthly years.

No motion has she now, no force;
She neither hears nor sees,
Rolled round in earth's diurnal course
With rocks and stones and trees!

Wordsworth married Mary Hutchinson in 1802. She was a childhood sweetheart. He as it were absolved this action by a visit to France to see Annette and his daughter Caroline on whom, when he was financially steady, he settled a small sum. He had been enthusiastic about the French Revolution in its early days. 'Bliss was it in that dawn to be alive', and indeed he and Coleridge had been mistaken for spies at the height of the war fever. Now he was appalled by the dictatorship of Napoleon, and this either coincided with or triggered off a general decline into a conservatism which deepened with age until the young

Robert Southey by
Peter Vandyke.

penniless romantic ended up as the archetypal Victorian Mountain of Morality
– against Reform Bills, railway lines and almost all democratic advance.

The Wordsworth who grew into a monument to be visited and looked at,
every bit as imposing as Skiddaw and Helvellyn, moved from one place to
another around Grasmere until he settled at Rydal Mount, where he lived in the
style of a gentleman of some means. Various inheritances and bequests, allied to
the tightest household management, meant that the money went a long way,
and there was the great irony of the last years when Wordsworth – now one to
cultivate the aristocracy he had railed against as a youth – became friends of
those very Lowthers whose meanness and use of the law had cheated his family
out of their rightful inheritance for so many crucial years.

Wordsworth's dedication to his work and to his high intentions was extraordinary. His income from poetry was minimal for years; some reviews were so
malevolent they would have crippled most writers; the critics and the town wits
had their day. But he kept on writing. Coleridge came up to Cumbria to join
him, and in the tracks of Coleridge came Southey – though again it has to be

217

stressed that it was a family connection and not a poetic mission which drew Southey north – however much he later became lumped together with the Lake Poets. Incidentally that description 'Lake Poets' was first employed in a damning review – and clearly not intended to applaud a sweet grouping.

Southey lived at Greta Hall and as time went on he and Wordsworth became friendly again. Their warm acquaintanceship of early manhood had been impaired by Southey's attack on Wordsworth's early poetry. Deaths in the family, illnesses, the common burden of Coleridge (he and Southey had married sisters) and an increasing similarity as they grew older – gravity, sobriety, conservatism, a sense of being mainstays of the established literature of the day – drew them closer together, and the embers of their old age glowed companionably together.

Southey's most quoted Lake District poem was composed for his children – the subject the Lodore Falls in Borrowdale.

> 'How does the Water
> Come down at Lodore?'
> My little boy ask'd me
> Thus, once on a time;
> And moreover he task'd me
> To tell him in rhyme.
> Anon at the word ...
>
> . . . .
>
> Retreating and beating and meeting and sheeting,
> Delaying and straying and playing and spraying,
> Advancing and prancing and glancing and dancing,
> Recoiling, turmoiling and toiling and boiling,
> And gleaming and streaming and steaming and beaming,
> And rushing and flushing and brushing and gushing,
> And flapping and rapping and clapping and slapping,
> And curling and whirling and purling and twirling,
> And thumping and plumping and bumping and jumping,
> And dashing and flashing and splashing and clashing;
> And so never ending, but always descending,
> Sounds and motions for ever and ever are blending,
> All at once and all o'er with mighty uproar,
> And this way the Water comes down at Lodore.

Wordsworth was indeed lucky in those who surrounded him. Not only did he

Lodore
Falls.

219

have, in Dorothy, someone who 'gave me eyes and gave me ears and humble cares and delicate fears', and in Coleridge the run of a mind as capacious as a well-stocked library; he had an admirer who at the age of seventeen trekked up from London to see him – was overcome by shyness, turned back – but came again to see and was conquered: Thomas de Quincey. That one of our very greatest essayists should settle in Grasmere (in Dove Cottage eventually) and leave us his own fine record of Wordsworth is the greatest luck. Here he describes his first meeting with his hero: he had accompanied Mr and Mrs Coleridge and Young Hartley, the boy prodigy.

In ascending this hill, from weariness of moving so slowly, I, with the two Coleridges, had alighted; and, as we all chose to refresh ourselves by running down the hill into Grasmere, we had left the chaise behind us, and had even lost the sound of the wheels at times, when all at once we came, at an abrupt turn of the road, in sight of a white cottage, with two yew-trees breaking the glare of its white walls. A sudden shock seized me on recognizing this cottage, of which, in the previous year, I had gained a momentary glimpse from Hammerscar, on the opposite side of the lake. I paused, and felt my old panic returning upon me; but just then, as if to take away all doubt upon the subject, I saw Hartley Coleridge, who had gained upon me considerably, suddenly turn in at a garden gate; this motion to the right at once confirmed me in my belief that here at last we had reached our port; that this little cottage was tenanted by that man whom, of all the men from the beginning of time, I most fervently desired to see; that in less than a minute I should meet Wordsworth face to face. Coleridge was of opinion that, if a man were really and consciously to see an apparition, in such circumstances death would be the inevitable result; and, if so, the wish which we hear so commonly expressed for such experience is as thoughtless as that of Semele in the Grecian Mythology, so natural in a female, that her lover should visit her en grand costume – presumptuous ambition, that unexpectedly wrought its own ruinous chastisement! Judged by Coleridge's test, my situation could not have been so terrific as his who anticipates a ghost; for, certainly, I survived this meeting; but at that instant it seemed pretty much the same to my own feelings.
Never before or since can I reproach myself with having trembled at the approaching presence of any creature that is born of woman, excepting only, for once or twice in my life, woman herself. Now, however, I did tremble; and I forgot, what in no other circumstances I could have forgotten, to stop for the coming up of the chaise, that I might be ready to hand Mrs Coleridge out. Had Charlemagne and all his peerage been behind me, or Caesar and his equipage, or Death on his pale horse, I should have forgotten them at that moment of intense expectation, and of eyes fascinated to what lay before me, or what might in a moment appear. Through the

Thomas de Quincey was one of Wordsworth's most fervent admirers; his account of his first meeting with the poet, recorded in *Recollection of the Lake Poets*, borders on hero-worship.

little gate I pressed forward; ten steps beyond it lay the principal door of the house. To this, no longer clearly conscious of my own feelings, I passed on rapidly; I heard a step, a voice, and, like flash of lightning, I saw the figure emerge of a tallish man, who held out his hand, and saluted me with most cordial expressions of welcome.

Yet again, De Quincey was supportive in those years when Wordsworth was so fiercely attacked. Hazlitt, too, has left us a record; over seventy painters left their record; later travellers, writers, diarists and journalists left us their impressions. The Wordsworth industry was under way well before his death.

Shelley came to live in the district for a few months and was deeply dismayed to find the young supporter of the Revolution changed into a cautious establishment figure. He said so – emphatically. Keats came too; but though he loved the poetry, he found the man pompous and boring. Charles Lamb was more kindly but nonetheless far from that circle of adoring supporters which surrounded Wordsworth with a praetorian ring of praise. Necessary, though, when so many outside the small circle of admirers ridiculed or ignored him for so long.

From the early nineteenth century onwards, it was almost *de rigueur* for writers to go to the Lakes and if possible see Wordsworth. The Americans came – Emerson, Hawthorne; Charlotte Brontë and Mrs Gaskell came; Christopher North settled there, as did Harriet Martineau and John Ruskin. All wrote something; some wrote memorable pieces. Keats wrote this account of a night spent in the Sun Inn at Ireby.

July 1st, 1818. We are this morning at Carlisle. After Skiddaw, we walked to Ireby, the oldest market town in Cumberland, where we were greatly amused by a country dancing-school, holden at the Sun. It was indeed "no new cotilion fresh from France". No, they Skip it and jump it with mettle extraordinary, and whisk it and frisk it and toed it and go'd it, and twirl'd it, and whirl'd it, and stamped it, and sweated it, tattooing the floor like mad. The difference between our country dances and these Scottish figures is about the same as leisurely stirring a cup of tea and beating up a batter-pudding.

I was extremely gratified to think that, if I had pleasures they knew nothing of, they had also something into which I could not possibly enter. I hope I shall not return without having got the Highland Fling. There was as fine a row of boys and girls as ever you saw. Some beautiful faces and one exquisite mouth. I never felt so near the glory of patriotism and the glory of making, by any means, a country happier. This is what I like better than scenery.

222

John Keats, sketched by B. R. Haydon.

Even Charles Dickens came to the Lakes. The metropolitan genius was not as impressed by the fells as he was supposed to be. This detail of his tour with Wilkie Collins and a local guide will warm the spirits of all who did not enjoy fell-walking.

Mr Goodchild looked eagerly at the top of the mountain, and, feeling apparently that he was now going to be very lazy indeed, shone all over wonderfully to the eye, under the influence of the contentment within and the moisture without. Only in the bosom of Mr Thomas Idle did Despondency now hold her gloomy state. He kept it a secret; but he would have given a very handsome sum, when the ascent began, to have been back again at the inn. The sides of Carrock looked fearfully steep, and the top of Carrock was hidden in mist. The rain was falling faster and faster. The knees of Mr Idle – always weak on walking excursions – shivered and shook with fear and damp. The wet was already penetrating through the young man's outer coat to a brand-new shooting-jacket, for which he had reluctantly paid the large sum of two guineas on leaving town; he had no stimulating refreshment about him but a small packet of clammy gingerbread nuts; he had nobody to give him an arm, nobody to push him gently behind, nobody to pull him up tenderly in front, nobody to speak to who really felt the difficulties of the ascent, the dampness of the rain, the denseness of the mist, and the unutterable folly of climbing, undriven, up any steep place in the world, when there is level ground within distance to walk on instead.

223

Was it for this that Thomas had left London? London, where there are nice short walks in level public gardens, with benches of repose set up at convenient distances for weary travellers; London, where rugged stone is humanely pounded into little lumps for the road, and intelligently shaped into smooth slabs for the pavement! No! It was not for the laborious ascent of the crags of Carrock that Idle had left his native city, and travelled to Cumberland. Never did he feel more disastrously convinced that he had committed a very grave error in judgement than when he found himself standing in the rain at the bottom of a steep mountain, and knew that the responsibility rested on his weak shoulders of actually getting up to the top of it.

At first the ascent was delusively easy, the sides of the mountain sloped gradually, and the material of which they were composed was a soft, spongy turf, very tender and pleasant to walk upon. After a hundred yards or so, however, the verdant scene and the easy slope disappeared, and the rocks began. Not noble, massive rocks, standing upright, keeping a certain regularity in their positions, and possessing, now and then, flat tops to sit upon, but little irritating, comfortless rocks, littered about anyhow by Nature; treacherous, disheartening rocks of all sorts of small shapes and small sizes, bruisers of tender toes and trippers-up of wavering feet. When these impediments were passed, heather and slough followed. Here the steepness of the ascent was slightly mitigated; and here the exploring party of three turned round to look at the view below them. The scene of the moorland and the fields was like a feeble water-colour drawing half sponged out. The mist was darkening, the rain was thickening, the trees were dotted about like spots of faint shadow, the division-lines which mapped out the fields, were all getting blurred together, and the lonely farm-house where the dog-cart had been left, loomed spectral in the grey light like the last human dwelling at the end of the habitable world.

Was this a sight worth climbing to see?

Surely – surely not! Up and up and then down a little and then up and then along a strip of level ground and then up again. The wind – a wind unknown in the happy valley – blows keen and strong. The rain mist gets impenetrable. A dreary little cairn of stones appears. The landlord adds one to the heap, first walking all round the cairn as if he were about to perform an incantation, then dropping the stone onto the top of the heap with the gesture of a magician adding an ingredient to a cauldron in full bubble. Good Charles sits down by the cairn as if it were his study table at home. Idle, drenched and panting, stands up with his back to the wind, ascertains distinctly that it *is* the top at last, looks round with all the little curiosity that is left in him, and gets in return a magnificent view of *nothing*.

Local men and men who became more local than the natives also took up their pens. Canon Rawnsley, surely the most prolific writer of sonnets in the history of literature, collected tales, wrote guides and histories and packed the place

Charles Dickens by
Daniel Maclise.

with prose. The local dialect has held firmly and surprisingly strongly. Of all the writers Robert Anderson, the Carlisle poet, though not strictly in the district, is the most distinguished of the dialect verifiers; and Thomas Farrall, who wrote under the pseudonym Betty Wilson, is the author of the loveliest dialect stories. I would like to represent the dialect here with a little-known poet, a short moving narrative from John Richardson (1817–86).

Ya winter neet, I mind it weel,
Oor lads 'ed been at t'fell,
An', bein'tir't, went seun to bed,
An' I sat be m'sell.
I hard a jike on t'window pane,
An' deftly went to see;
Bit when I ax't, 'Who's jikin theer?'
Says t'chap, 'It's nobbut me.'

'Who's me?' says I, 'What want you here?
Oor fwok ur aw i'bed' –

225

'I dunnet want your fwok at aw,
It's thee I want,' he sed.
'What cant'e want wi' me,' says I;
'An' who, the deuce, can't be?
Jest tell me who it is, an' then' –
Says he, 'It's nobbut me.'

'I want a sweetheart, an' I thowt
Thoo mebby wad an' aw;
I'd been a bit down t'deal to-neet,
An' thowt' at I wad caw;
What, cant'e like me, dus t'e think?
I think I wad like thee' –
'I dunnet know who 't is,' says I,
Says he, 'It's nobbut me.'

We pestit on a canny while,
I thowt his voice I kent;
An' than I steall quite whisht away,
An' oot at t'dooer I went.
I creapp, an' gat 'im be t'cwoat laps,
'Twas dark, he cuddent see;
He startit roond, an' said, 'Who's that?'
Says I, 'It's nobbut me.'

An' menny a time he com agean,
An' menny a time I went,
An' sed, 'Who's that 'at's jiken theer?'
When gaily weel I kent:
An' mainly what t'seamm answer com,
Fra back o't'laylick tree;
He sed, 'I think thoo knows who't is:
Thoo knows it's nobbut me.'

It's twenty year an' mair sen than,
An' ups an' doons we've hed;
An' six fine barns hev blest us beath,
Sen Him an' me war wed.
An' menny a time I've known 'im steal,
When I'd yan on me knee,

To make me start, an' than wad laugh –
'Ha! Ha! It's nobbut me.'

But the most moving local work I came across was in an oral history compiled by Elizabeth Roberts. Here, a woman remembers one of her mother's pregnancies at the end of the nineteenth century.

She never told us a word, we knew nothing then . . . We used to know how fat mam was getting but we didn't know anything. Then I heard a noise one night and I got up and I thought m'mamma must be bad and I went in the room and said, "Is mamma bad?" Dad said, "No go and get yourself back into bed m'lass she'll be all right till morning". When I got up in the morning and went in she had this little baby and it was stillborn. She said, "You're not going to school today Rose". I said. "Aren't I?" She said, "No you'll have to stay at home I want you to do something for me". I said, "What's been the matter with you mamma?" She said, "Well I've got a baby". I said "Where is it?" She said, "It's just there", and it was on a wash stand, on a pillow with a cover over it. When I looked at it it was like a little doll, very small. She said, "I want you to go to a shop and ask for a soap box". I said, "A soap box mam". She said, "Yes". I said, "What's it for?" She said, "To put that baby in".

I brought this soap box back and I called on the road to my friend, a girl I went with, so I told her and she went with me. She said, "I'll come down to your house with you".

She came and we had a look at this little doll and my friend said, "Let us line this little box with wadding". We lined this box with this bit of wadding and then m'mamma put this wee baby in it, and the lid fastened down like the boxes do today – no nails. She gave me a letter. "Now you've got to go up the cemetery and give this letter to the grave digger, any grave digger you see in". I said, "I can't take it wrapped up in paper". So I went in the back and saw an old coat of m'dad's. I ripped the black lining out of this coat and we wrapped this little box in this lining and put some string round it, put it under our arms and off we went to the grave digger. I give him this letter and he read it. He said, "Oh yes, just take it over in the church porch, you'll see a few parcels in that corner, just leave it there". Me, being inquisitive, said, "What are you going to do with it?" He said, "Well we'll have public graves, everybody doesn't buy graves, they don't have the money, when the public graves get nearly full up, we put one in each grave". "Oh, that's what you do," I said. He said, "Yes, tell your Mammy it'll be alright". And we turned back home.

Beatrix Potter came to the Lakes, and stayed to write books which seem as destined for immortality as some of Wordsworth's poems. Her journals are like those of Dorothy Wordsworth in their attention to local detail.

I had a long talk with the postmistress, a lame girl on crutches. I went afterwards to see Miss Hanes in an old row of cottages above the Sky Hill – a little, thin, elderly woman with black hair and eyes, in spectacles, with a clean cottage and soapy hands.

I heard a long history of her daughter Jane, a girl to whom we took a great fancy, which seems to have been mutual unless butter entered into our conversation. I heard the history of Jane not marrying a coachman who took to drinking, and lost his place after the banns were put up; but the queer part of it was the way the course of events was taken, not as a disappointment but as a positive success, in the very nick of time, and he had turned out so very badly since.

Then I turned to cats, caats, a he "cart", a black Persian named Sadi whom we had bestowed on Jane. I should fail to give an impression of old Mrs Hanes looking over her spectacles and gesticulating in the middle of the flagged kitchen, nor would the joke be perceived without previous knowledge of Sadi, whom I saw last as a splendid half-grown kitten of diabolical temperament.

"He wad stand on the table and clar ye", she thought the world of that caat. Also he was "moross" which I can well believe from what I saw of him.

When they took him to Liverpool he led them a dance. Jane wad be up ladders and over walls. Mrs Goodison thought the world of that caat. Mr Goodison didn't. It used to go to sleep in his arm chair and he was afraid to stir it. It was a trojan. It died of a consumption when it was only three.

I walked after lunch as far as Tent Lodge, and much regretted I could not go on to Coniston Bank to see Barnes and especially Mrs Barnes, a fine old Cumberland farmer's wife, homely and comely. We drove home by Yewdale and Skelwith.

Saturday, August 10th. In the afternoon went with the pony up Troutbeck and put it up at the Mortal Man which looks a very nice little inn. Papa and I walked up Nanny Lane and got over a stile into the heather, sweet and heavy with honey. There was a thunder-haze, no view, but very peaceful, except that the stone walls were covered with flying-ants.

I did not find many fossils, but we had great pleasure watching a pair of buzzards sailing round and round over the top of Wansfell. There was an old shepherd half way up the side of Troutbeck, much bent and gesticulating with a stick. He watched the collie scouring round over stone walls, coming close past us without taking the slightest notice. Four or five sheep louped over a wall at least three feet high on our right and escaped the dog's observation, whereupon the ancient shepherd, a mere speck in the slanting sunlight down the great hillside, this aged Wordsworthian worthy, awoke the echoes with a flood of the most singularly bad language. He gesticulated and the dog ran round on the top of dykes, and some young cattle ran down with their tails in the air.

It is most curious how sound travels up either side of the steep Troutbeck valley, but in keeping to be greeted with the classical but not time-honoured phrase

The ideas for Beatrix Potter's stories often appeared first in picture-letters to the children of friends. This example was written in the Lake District.

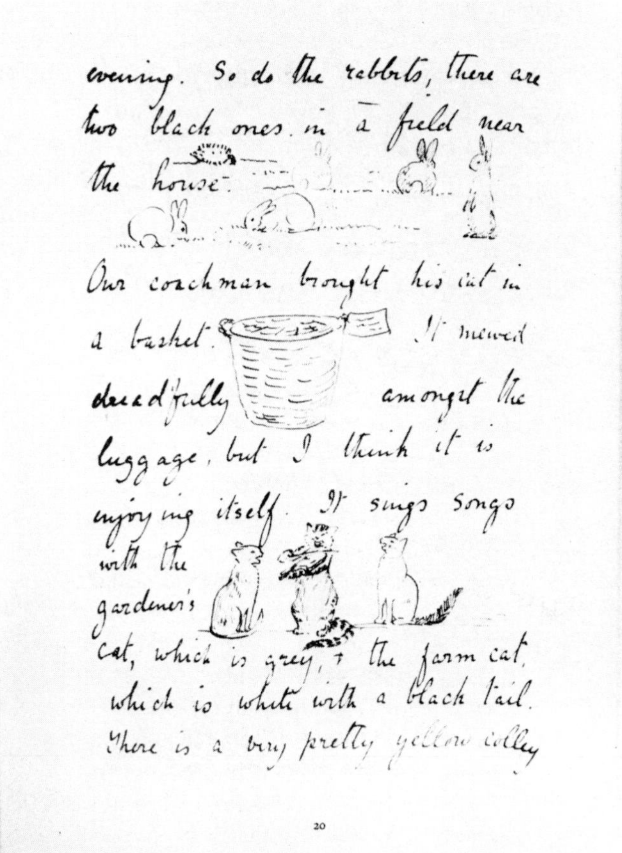

evening. So do the rabbits, there are two black ones in a field near the house. Our coachman brought his cat in a basket. It mewed dreadfully amongst the luggage, but I think it is enjoying itself. It sings songs with the gardener's cat, which is grey, + the farm cat, which is white with a black tail. There is a very pretty yellow collie

20

addressed by La Pucelle to invaders. We passed him sitting on a wall as we came down, a pleasant, smiling old fellow. We asked him which was Ill Bell and he leant over the wall, "Ye'll perceive I'm rather hard of hearing", then heard that the prize-pup at Kelso Show was named "Sandy Walker".

Her home at Sawrey is the most visited home in the Lakes. There are fears that the numbers are now so great the place is threatened with erosion!

Arthur Ransome of *Swallows and Amazons* kept a not dissimilar record of his childhood visits to Coniston, and the historian W. G. Collingwood also rhapsodised his youth in the Lakes. In the century following Wordsworth the idea that good could come from living in and looking at nature became not so much a fashion as a faith.

229

In this century, Hugh Walpole used the place as a setting for his epic family saga – *The Herries Chronicle* – which, in its day, was received with the highest acclaim. Today there are still many Walpole-lovers who follow the paths of his heroes and heroines up around Watendlath.

Graham Sutton has written numerous novels set in the area and the poetry of Norman Nicholson has drawn sturdily from the place in which he was born. His 'Sea to the West' is squarely in Wordsworth's tradition, and yet it speaks clearly of Nicholson himself, of a man who has lived on Cumbria's western coast and loved its fells and valleys all his life.

When the sea's to the west
The evenings are one dazzle –
You can find no sign of water,
Sun upflows the horizon;
Waves of shine
Heave, crest, fracture,
Explode on the shore;
The wide day burns
In the incandescent mantle of the air.

Once, fifteen,
I could lean on handlebars,
Staring into the flare,
Blinded by looking,
Letting the gutterings and sykes of light
Flood into my skull.

Then, on the stroke of bedtime,
I'd turn to the town,
Cycle past purpling dykes
To a brown drizzle
Where black scum shadows
Stagnated between backyard walls.
I pulled the warm dark over my head
Like an eiderdown.

Yet in that final stare when I
(Five times perhaps, fifteen)
Creak protesting away –

Sir Hugh Walpole by Stephen Bone.

The sea to the west,
The land darkening –
Let my eyes at the last be blinded
Not by the dark
But by dazzle.

Wordsworth is still the supreme literary presence in the Lakes. He has been out of fashion and in again; his clumsiness has been ridiculed; some of his subjects and lines are so banal they take your breath away; but nothing can stand in the light of his greatness as a poet. For him and through him alone the place will live as long as those with 'thinking hearts' care to read.

And O, ye Fountains, Meadows, Hills, and Groves,
Forebode not any severing of our loves!
Yet in my heart of hearts I feel your might;
I only have relinquished one delight
To live beneath your more habitual sway.

231

I love the Brooks which down their channels fret,
Even more than when I tripped lightly as they;
The innocent brightness of a new-born Day
Is lovely yet;
The Clouds that gather round the setting sun
Do take a sober colouring from an eye
That hath kept watch o'er man's mortality;
Another race hath been, and other palms are won.
Thanks to the human heart by which we live,
Thanks to its tenderness, its joys, and fears,
To me the meanest flower that blows can give
Thoughts that do often lie too deep for tears.

Epilogue

The best way to enter Cumbria still is to walk across the bay from Morecambe to Grange-over-Sands. As you get to the middle of the – guided – journey, perhaps that early thrill of horror which spiced the visits of the first tourists will overcome you as you remember the disasters which have overcome some previous travellers on these sands. But Black Combe will beckon, solid old Black Combe girding the southern reach of Lakeland; and the unexpected Edwardian elegance of Grange-over-Sands, with its tasteful gardens along the promenade, its plant life more Cornish than Cumbrian, its permeating sense of security, will provide a safe harbour.

The next stop would be two or three miles away, at Cartmel, whose village centre, with its charming clutter of houses from the three last centuries, its arches and side streets, can fairly claim to be the prettiest in the whole district. As if that were not enough, there is the Norman Priory church with its droll misericords and double tower which gives it a unique Lakeland flourish. For the profane, there's a lovely little racecourse just behind the square – and with a splendidly rummagy bookshop and cheerful pubs, Cartmel adds up to a place for all tastes and seasons.

That part of Cumbria south of Windermere has always been comparatively neglected. Norman Nicholson's loyalties to Millom and the Duddon Valley have laid down treasures for the future; if or when the fashion for appreciating industrial archaeology grows, Millom could become a period piece. Certainly it shows off to the greatest advantage that touching contrast which characterizes so much of those parts of Britain early and heavily industrialized: machinery, and urban concentration on the dirty work of hacking out ore, set against spectacular countryside. Who knows? Those factories and pit heads – now that they are lost to the burden of labour which sustained them – do have an

attraction: the pyramids, after all, maintain their splendour despite the knowledge that many thousands of slaves must have wasted their lives in hauling that
stone into place. The first world industrial revolution did begin and once
flourished in this country; as we slide uncertainly towards the future, that
inheritance might serve us a second time and become an open museum.

In which case, Barrow-in-Furness will be worth the trip. I have an affection
for Barrow which might be the British inclination to veer towards the underdog.
For, stuck down there in the heel of Cumbria, this town, totally created for
industry, draws in few tourists and excites fewer rhapsodies. I like the surprise
of the place. It was constructed – in that lovely local sandstone – in one great
whirl of self-confidence – to be not only a place of work but a city of splendour.
The streets are broad; the institutional buildings would delight John Betje-
man's love of the Victorian; that imperial architecture surrounding the ship-
yards is undoubtedly impressive – there it stands, full of power, inventions,
people's working effort. While across on Walney Island, the wild life and traces
of very earliest settlement exist beside the beating of the sea against a coastline
which finds it hard to resist erosion. There is an optimism from our entrepreneurial past, and a Tennysonian melancholy, about Barrow and the Isle of
Walney which makes its mood unique. Other industrial towns up the coast –
Whitehaven with its grid system and late Georgian housing – the coal-sea
villages up through Workington to Maryport with the neat, attractive harbour
subject of so many prints and paintings – this industrial cordon which has drawn
out so much humankind from the Lake District is worth considering as the alter
ego of the place; the other side of the moon. But Barrow stands supreme and, as
if to crown the argument, there is its wonderful Cistercian abbey, best seen in its
blood-red ruins just before sunset.

Ulverston is much more 'Lakeland' than Barrow. The centre of the town is a
delight for anyone who enjoys that felicitous jumble of styles and buildings
serving different purposes. Here, as in Keswick, Cockermouth, Penrith and
Wigton, the time to go is market day, when the streets reclaim the life of barter
and concourse which suit them so well and the farmers come in to trade with
their cattle, sheep and pigs. Nearby Broughton in Furness, which no longer
has its market, is a museum piece. The eighteenth-century square, with its
clock which still chimes the hours, and stone slabs, relics of sale and trade,
stands as peaceful as somewhere lightly touched by sleep in a fairy tale. To stand
there on a sunny morning – as I did some months ago – is to feel a childlike sense
of time ticking away without effect. There are villages galore in the relatively

unexplored area of Furness, few to equal Urswick for its compact thirteenth-century church and the pre-Norman fortifications nearby.

Churches with a leper's window, grandiose follies suddenly on a bare hill-top, fine nineteenth-century houses protected by their parkland acres, ancient settlements – you can drive around the southernmost part of this district without a dull mile. It is at Bowness-on-Windermere that Lakeland culture in its public sense begins.

There are the boats moored, ready to take you around Belle Island or up to Ambleside; the ranks of confident Victorian hotels which sprang up to accommodate the visitors arriving by rail after 1847; the woods and walks beside the shore. Bowness-on-Windermere, like Keswick, has suffered in fashion because of its popularity: a common consequence.

Bowness in the south and Keswick on the saddle of land between Derwent Water and Bassenthwaite in the north are almost twin towns in respect of the numbers drawn in during the holiday season and the highly developed way in which the urban economy is directed towards tourism. Bowness is more handsome; Keswick more fetching with its Moot Hall and parks, the museum with the singing stones and the Century Theatre. Both are at their best between September and April when the presence of the lakes and the atmosphere of the slated buildings can quickly permeate the spirit of the place.

Between those two tourist centres are three other battered spots: Ambleside, Grasmere and Hawkshead. Ambleside, at the head of Windermere, takes up the spa feeling of Bowness, but the flow of people and traffic is easily avoided by stepping across into the parks which swing around to Rydal Water. That easy route, extended around the back of Rydal, has a peacefulness about it which is as distinctive as any other walk I have ever taken in the Lakes. Down in Grasmere, all you want to do is to join the local trusts which are fighting to preserve it. Grasmere needs a long convalescence from the visitors who tread through Dove Cottage and drive on into the village for gifts; and yet it seems churlish to complain. On quiet days, its setting and simple village organization makes it one of the most charming villages of all: worthy of Wordsworth's devotion. Over in Hawkshead, the Wordsworth industry has brought about its only real casualty – a car park so big and so prominently placed that it threatens to destroy entirely the mood of the place. I remember Hawkshead before the car park. A magical village of archways, courtyards, outside steps, squares, higgledy-piggledy yet retaining stern traces of its fame as a woollen town with the idiosyncratic Church of St Michael and All Angels crowning it perfectly. It was one of those places which could make you believe in psychic phenomena – so crowded with vibrations of contentment. Still, despite the car park, the Grammar School has to be seen to be believed, and the *correct* cottage in which Wordsworth lodged has to be visited. There can be no other writer in history as well served by the buildings which bred, educated and housed him.

Outside the main markers, the thing to do is to wander at will – up into the Langdales; up Borrowdale to Seathwaite; down into Eskdale; over to Appleby which can boast the most spectacular main street in the area, hurtling down from the twelfth-century castle to St Lawrence's from the same century, past tiny cottages and handsome eighteenth-century town houses; to Bewcastle and Gosforth for the crosses; to Buttermere for that unique sense of cul-de-sac calm; to Dacre for the castle, and the four famous bears in the churchyard; to Cockermouth for that most handsome of main streets, and the grandest Wordsworth house of all; to Lorton for the yews; all over the district there are towns, villages and hamlets which vary and continue the careful complexities of the landscape.

The social cat's cradle is constantly netted and unravelled: the teams and institutes, the shows and sports, Appleby Gypsy Fair, Egremont's Crab Apple Fair, Wigton's Horse Fair, the Shepherd's Meet in Wasdale, the conventions which gather still near Derwentwater and baptize their members in the lake the Celts named 'white water'. On the tops the park rangers restore the damage done; in the valleys the land is intensively farmed; the place has a hum of modest prosperity and the feeling that it serves people well.

In the Northern Fells, where I live, there is more hardiness about the landscape. Villages like Ireby, Uldale and Hesket Newmarket are work-a-day places and it is that I suppose which principally attracted me to this particular area. It was here that I began to think of this book and began the reading and visiting necessary for the writing of it.

Now it is done, I feel that I know much better something I have 'known' all the time. In Ireby, it is rare to find a local man who has visited the wider district at all extensively: it is as if they disdained the effort, believing that what they know so well in microcosm is wealth enough and needed no topping up. I, having left the place for ten years, enjoy the exploration of what is so near. Yet when the compass has swung around in its circle, the point at the centre remains more significant than the line which has been drawn, and that feeling of being part of a place because you have invested your life there is one whose certainty can rise above all the many reasons and explanations for loving it. Of course,

236

The station whence he looked was soft and green,
Not giddy yet aerial, with a depth
Of vale below, a weight of hills above.

William Wordsworth, 'The Recluse'.

Today, Grasmere needs a long convalescence from the visitors who tread through Dove Cottage and drive into the village for gifts. . . .

now, I feel enriched by some knowledge of the age of the rocks, the displacement of castles and keeps, the 'stations' which were pilgrim points for the early tourists, the sites of legends, the hillsides of battles, the marks of old workings, the traces of ancient field systems. In that sense, this has been a journey towards knowledge. Nor am I embarrassed to declare that several times – though not as often as when I was younger – I have experienced that deep fulfilment of the senses which comes unexpectedly in some lonely spot and seems to speak of a

A Bronze Age circle and the atomic plant at Sellafield.

profound relationship with what is all around: with the rocks and stones and trees, with the water and winds and the changing screens of light. We *are* part of a natural world; perhaps, at times, that natural world is available to our deepest memories.

What this place has is an enduring and mysterious certainty. Those hills, you feel, will never change – certainly not in any foreseeable lifetime; the lakes may turn into reservoirs, the villages may become dormitories or ghostly clusters of old houses, that bold line of industry down the west coast is already thinning to a mere tracing of industrial remains; but there is still that which Wordsworth and Turner saw in the hills – a sense of permanence. A comfort, in its way, however false any praise of permanence might seem now; however mocking it sounds in the presence of so many uncertainties; however useless that permanence is – for what comfort can there be in range after range of bare-backed fells? Yet they are the core of the place. From where I live I can walk for a few minutes and look over to Skiddaw where the adventure began so many millions of years ago. Down on the coast around the buff where the old coalfields sank into the sea is Windscale – unfortunate symbol of the nuclear age – an age which could end it all in the way the Book of Revelations prophesizes. Yet, you feel, though this *might* be so, at some level under the ashes, under the silt and debris, forces such as those which raised Skiddaw long before we were imagined, would start again and another adventure would begin, here in Cumbria.

Acknowledgements

Page numbers in **bold** type indicate colour illustrations.

BBC Hulton Picture Library: 81 (right); K. Benson: 22; Geoffrey Berry: 8, 9, 10 (left), 13, 15, 17, 19, 23, 26, 28, 29, 47, 49, 51, 52, 53 (left), 74, 78, 80 (above), 92 (below), 116, 119, 121, 155, 156, 157, 164, 166, 167, 168 (above and below), 236, 237; British Library: **87**; British Museum: 32, 153; Simon Crouch: **162, 203, 207-8**; Cumberland and Westmorland Antiquarian and Archaeological Society: 57; Cumbria County Library, Barrow: 21, 58, 59, 63, 71, 131, 137 (above and below), 152, 163; Cumbria County Library, Carlisle: 114, 188, 189, 190; Cumbria County Record Office: 130 (Barrow), 138 (Kendal), 143 (Carlisle); Cumbrian Newspapers Group Ltd: 96–9; Norman Duerden: **35, 36, 38–9, 40, 41, 42, 67, 159** (above and below), **160, 204, 205, 208**; E. T. Archive: **141** (above); A. J. Finn: **37, 209, 210**; Fitz Park Museum: 6, 129; David W. Jones: 80 (below), 82, 93, 100, 103, 110, 113 (right), 115; Mansell Collection: 86 (left and right); Bob Matthews: 48, **160**, 165; J. Melville: 79 (below); W. R. Mitchell: 92 (above), 125; National Portrait Gallery: 134, 154 (right), 158, **161** (above and below), 169, 217, 223, 225, 229, 231; J. W. Parker: 68; W. Rollinson: 24, 33, 34, 43, 55 (left and right), **70**, 76, 87, 101; Royal Aircraft Establishment, Farnborough: 4; The Society of Antiquaries of London: 55 (above); Mrs A. E. Smith and the late Ralph Cross: 27; Mrs Jane Smith: 79 (above); Alan Spain: **69**; Tate Gallery: **139**; University of Cambridge Committee for Aerial Photography: 45; Crown Copyright Victoria and Albert Museum: 85, 127; Victoria and Albert Museum and Sally Chappell: **140** (above); Jean Ward and Dennis Harding: 44, 46; Westmorland Gazette: 132; The Yorkshire Museum: 53 (right).

The author and publishers would also like to thank Abbot Hall Art

Gallery and Museum of Lakeland Life and Industry, Kendal, Cumbria, for the use of the following illustrations: 10 (right), 171, 172, 173, 174, 177, all of which were made available from the Abraham Collection by courtesy of the Fell and Rock Climbing Club of the English Lake District; 54 (left and right), courtesy of Kendal Museum of Natural History and Archaeology; 25, 30, 77, 81 (left), 113 (left), courtesy of the Museum of Lakeland Life and Industry, Abbot Hall, Kendal; **90** (above), **141** (below), 181, 183 (above), courtesy of Abbot Hall Art Gallery, Kendal; **140** (below), 196, courtesy of Abbot Hall Art Gallery, Kendal (A. S. Clay Collection); **88** (above), **89** (below), **90** (below), 136, **142** (above), 182, 183 (below), 184, 191, 192 (below), courtesy of private collections; **88** (below), 186, Tyne and Wear Museums; 179, The Trustees of the Clonterbrook Settlement; 192 (above), Victoria and Albert Museum; 194, Ferens Art Gallery, City of Kingston upon Hull; 195, Leeds City Art Galleries and Museums.

Illustrations on pp. 212–13 and 221 are reproduced by permission of the Trustees of Dove Cottage.

The illustration on p. 229 is reproduced by permission of Frederick Warne Ltd, from *The History of the Writings of Beatrix Potter*, compiled by Leslie Linder.

The Sea to the West, Norman Nicholson, copyright © Faber & Faber, 1981. Extract from *The Journal of Beatrix Potter*, transcribed by Leslie Linder, copyright © Frederick Warne PLC.

Index

Numbers in in italics refer to illustrations.

Abraham brothers of Keswick, *172*,
  173–4, 175, 191
Addingham Cross, 52
Aethelfrith, 51–2
Aethelred the Unready, 56
Agricola, 47
Aira Force, 122, *123*
Allerdale above Derwent, 57
Allerdale below Derwent, 57
Ambleside, 28, 48, 49, 54, *195*, 235
  paintings of, *142*, 184, *184*, 190, 195,
    195
  Roman fort (Galava), 48, *48*, 50
  rush bearing, 130
  sports, 106, 117
  tourism, 154
Appleby, 57, 60, 236
  Gypsy Fair, 236
  market, 57
Armathwaite Hall, 153
Arnside, 54
Ashness Bridge, 26
Askham Fell, 33
Aspatria, 51, 54, 102, 187
Aughertree Fell, enclosures at, *44*
Austen, Jane, 150

Barrow-in-Furness, 234
  Cistercian abbey, 234
Bassenthwaite, *209*, 235
Beaker People, 33–4, 43
Beckermet, 20
Bede, the Venerable, 52, 118
Belle Isle, Windermere, 235
  Round House on, *152*, 153, *153*

Bellers, William, 188
  'View of Skiddaw and
    Derwentwater', 188–9, *190*
Bewcastle Cross, 52, *52*, 236
Birker, 54
Black Combe, 7, 9, 233
Blacklock, William Jones, 185–6
  'Catbells and Cawsey Pike' by,
    186
Blaeu map (1645), 136
Blencathra, or Saddleback, 7, 22, 24,
  44
bobbin industry, 92, *93*, 94
Bodleian map (1300), 57, *57*
Borrowdale, 14, 45, 140, *140*, *186*, *191*,
  236
  Bowder Stone, *146*
  Castle Crag, 45, *140*, 195
  graphite industry, 85
  Gray's account of visit to, 145–6
  Lodore Falls, *179*, 181, 218, *219*,
    220
  paintings of, 180, 181, *186*, 187, 188,
    195
Borrowdale Volcanics, 8–9, 10, *10*
Bough, Sam, 186–7, *186*, 189
Bowder Stone, Borrowdale, *146*
Bowen map, 138
Bowles map, 138
Bowness-on-Windermere, 235
Brampton, 57
Brandlehow Mine, Derwent Water, *91*
Brantwood, Coniston, 157
Bridekirk font, *69*
Brigantes, 46–7, 48

Brigham, 53
  crosses, 52, 54
Brigham, near Keswick, 86
Broad Stand, Scafell, *171*
Brockhole, Windermere, 165, *165*
Bromfield, 51
Brontë, Charlotte, 222
Bronze Age, 31, 33, *238*
Brougham, 48
Broughton in Furness, 234
buildings, 27–8
  Celtic round huts and hill forts, 45
  cruck-timbered barn, Field Head
    Farm, *27*
  farmsteads, 27–8, *76*, 78, *159*
  mansions (nineteenth-century),
    152, 153, *155*, *156*
  Norman castles and monasteries,
    57, *58*, 58–9, *59*, 60, *60*
  Roman forts and bath-house, 47, 48,
    48, *49*, 49–50, 68
  'Statesmen's' houses, *83*, *84*, 84–5
  Wasdale Head village school, *71*
Burell Green, 'Luck' of, 127
Burgh by Sands, 57
Buttermere, 14, *42*, 126, 236

Caermote, 48
Caldbeck, 22, 43, 51
  bobbin mill, *92*
Caledonian earth-movement, 12
Camden, William, 134
  Britannia, 133
Carboniferous Limestone, 11, *41*
Carlisle, 31, 57, 95, 186
  Augustinian priory, 59
  Castle, 31, 57
  Cathedral, 54
  Cross, 52
  Hiring Fair, *81*
Carnforth, 171
Carrington map, 138
Carrock Fell, 11, 18
  Iron Age hill fort, 45, *46*
Cartmel, 31, *100*, 233
Cartmel Fell, St Anthony's Chapel,
  204
castle(s), 57, 60
  Carlisle, 31, 57
  Dacre, 60, *60*
  Egremont, 57, *58*
  Penrith, *59*
  Sizergh, *205*

  Wray, *155*
Castle Crag, Borrowdale, 45, *140*, 195
Castlerigg Stone Circle, 34, *34*, *160*
  legends about, 124
Cat Bells, *119*
Celts (Cymry), 43–5
Christianity, 50, 51, 52, 54, 118, 129
Cistercians, 21, 76, 234
Clappersgate, *141*
Clarke, Hexham, wrestler, *106*
Coal Measures, 11
coalmining, 21, 86, 91, 94
Cockermouth, 95, *206–7*, 236
  Castle, 14, 57
  market, 57
  Wordsworth in, 197, 198, 236
Cocker, River, 14
Coleridge, Hartley, 220
Coleridge, Samuel Taylor, *169*, 198,
  201, 216, 217, 220
  descent of Scafell by, 169–70, *171*
Collingwood, W. G., 2, 49, *49*, 51, 83,
  193, 229
  and family, 193
Collins, Wilkie, 223
Company of Mines Royal, 85, *86*, *91*
Coniston, 9, 13, 157, 179
  Fells, *37*
  fishing, *167*
  Turner's paintings of, *139*, 179–80
  Yewtree Farm and 'spinning
    gallery', *159*
Coniston Foxhounds, *115*
Coniston Hall, 153
Coniston Limestone, 10
Coniston Water, 59, 75
Constable, John, 180, 182, 195
  'The Cascade, Rydal', *181*
  'Falls of Lodore', 181
  'Langdale Pikes', *182*
  'Morning – Borrowdale', 180
  'Storm over Derwentwater –
    Evening', *140*, 180–81
copper, copper mining, 27, 32, 85
Crinkle Crags, 8, *8*
Crosby Ravensworth, 43
crosses:
  Anglian, 52, *52–3*
  Bewcastle, 52, *52*
  Gosforth, 54, *55*, 56
  Irton, 52, *53*
  Norse, 54, *55*, 56
Crosthwaite, 51, 54, 145

242

Crosthwaite, Peter, maps of, 150, *151*
Crummock Water, 14
Cuthbert, St, 52, 118

Dacre:
    Castle, 60, *60*, 236
    Cross, 52
Dalton-in-Furness, 185
Dash Beck, 7
Dash Farm, Skiddaw, *209*
David de Brugings, 106
De Quincey, Thomas:
    first meeting with Wordsworth, 220, *221*, 222
    Recollection of the Lake Poets, 121–2
Dearham, 53
    Cross, 54
Defoe, Daniel, 134, *134*, 135–6
Derwent Isle, 150, *151*
Derwent, River, 14, 199
Derwent Water, 118, *119*, 150, 180–81, 188, 235
    paintings and engravings of, *136*, 180–81, 188, *189*, *190*
Devoke Water, *90*
Dickens, Charles, *225*
    tour of the Lakes by, 223–4
Dove Cottage, 165, 197, 202, 220, 235, *237*
Drigg, 31
Druids, 44, 124
dry-stone walls, 25, 25–6, 78, *160*
Duddon, Duddon valley, 14, 33, 233

Eamont Bridge, 32
Ecgfrith, King, 52
Edenhall, 'Luck' of, 126–7, *127*
Eden Valley, 33
Edmund, King, 56
Edward I, King, 58
Egremont, 14
    Castle, 57, *58*
    Crab Apple Fair, 236
    market, 57
Ehenside Tarn, 32
Elterwater, 9
Embleton, 27, 44
Emerson, Ralph Waldo, 222
enclosures, Iron Age, *44*, *45*
engravings/prints, 178, 179, 187–91, 193, 194
Ennerdale, 14, 25
    chapels, 59, 76
    forestry, *23*

gatnering sheep for dipping, *78*
Esk, River, 14
Eskdale, 11, 14, 59, 170, 171, 236
    upper, *13*, 59
Eskdale and Ennerdale Hunt, 113
Ethelred of York, 54
Eveling, King, 49

farmhouses, farmsteads, 27–8, *76*, 78, *83*
farming, 30, 32, 75–86, 91, 95
    broadcasting seed, *81*
    Celtic, 44
    enclosure movement, 77–8
    hiring fair, *81*
    mechanization, 78
    monks' development of, 75–6
    rotation of crops, 77
    sheep, 21, 75, *78–80*, *82*
    shows, *80*, *81*
    the 'Statesmen', 83–5
    threshing, *77*, *79*
Fell, Sheila, 178, 187
Fell and Rock Climbing Club, 174
fells, 22, 24
    dry-stone walling, *25*, 25–6
    re-afforestation, 24–5
    see also farming
Field Head Farm, Hawkshead, 27
    cruck-timbered barn, *27*
Fiennes, Hon. Celia, 133–4
fishing, fisheries, 75, 167, *167*
forests, 18–19, 21–2
    hunting in, 58
    re-afforestation, 24–5
forts, hill:
    Celtic, 45
    Iron Age, 45, *46*
    Roman, 47–8, *48*, 49–50, *51*, 68
    Viking, 56
fox-hunting, 112–14
Friar's Crag, 157, 184
Frizington, 11, 53
funeral traditions and superstitions, 129, 130, *130*, 131
Furness, 12, 235
    St Mary's Abbey, 59, *70*, 75, *87*, 124
Furness Morris Men, *100*

Galava (Ambleside), 48
Gaskell, Mrs Elizabeth, 222
'the Giant's Grave', Penrith churchyard, 52
Gibson, Richard 'the Dwarf', 185

243

Gilpin, Rev. William (1724–1804), *89*, 147–8, 150, 189, 190, 198
Gilpin, William (1733–1807), animal painter, 185
Gimmer Crag, Great Langdale, *10*
Glannaventa (Ravenglass), 49
Glaramara, 32
Gosforth Church, *55*
Gosforth Cross, 54, *55*, 56, 236
Gowbarrow Park, Ullswater, daffodils at, *67*
Grange-in-Borrowdale, *85*
  bridge, 26, *26*
Grange-over-Sands, 11, *41*, 155, 233
granite, granite quarrying, 11, 16, 27, 85
graphite industry, 85
Grasmere, 3, 14, 16, 24, 29, 31, *37*, *141*, 220, 235, *237*
  rush bearing, 130, *131*, *132*
  tourism, 154
  Wordsworth in, 197, 202, 217
Grasmere Sports, 106, *106*, 107, 117
Grasmoor hills, 7
Graves, John Woodcock, 113, *114*
Gray, Thomas, 144–6, 150, 198
Great Gable (Gavel), *10*, 12, 13, 14, 16, 18, *35*, *177*
Great Langdale, *10*, 18, 27
  broadcasting seed, *81*
  footpath, *168*
Green, William, *89*, 184, *184*, 190–91, *192*
Greta Hall (Southey's home), 218
Grizedale, 24
Grizedale Forest, 11

Hadrian, Emperor, 48
Hadrian's Wall, 50
haematite quarrying, 27
Hankinson, Alan, 174
  The First Tigers, 171–3
Harden, John, of Brathay Hall, *141*, 195–6, *196*
Hardknott Roman fort, 48, 49–50, *51*, *68*
Harter Fell, 49, *51*, 124
Harter Fell Andesites, 9
Haskett Smith, Perry, 172, 173, *173*, 174
Hatfield, John (alias Hon. Colonel Hope), *125*
Hawes, 124

Haweswater, 14, 16, *157*
Hawkshead, 11, 27, 235–6
  Church of St Michael and All Angels, 235
  Grammar School, 76, 197, 199, 236
Hawthorne, Nathaniel, 222
Haydon, B. R., *161*
Hazlitt, William, 222
Heaton Cooper, Alfred, 193
Heaton Cooper family of painters, 193
Helvellyn, 14, *164*
Hensingham, 53
Herbert, St, legend of, 118
Hercynian earth-movements, 12
Hesket Newmarket, 236
Heversham Cross, 52
Hewthwaite Hall, date stone over door, *84*
High Nibthwaite, 150
High Pike, 9
High Street (Roman road), 22, *47*, 48
Hodge Close slate quarry, *208*
Hodgkinson, Joseph, and Donald, Thomas, map of, 143, *143*
Holm Cultram monastery, 59
Honister, 9
Honister Crag, *148*
Honister slate quarries, *203*
Honorius, Emperor, 50
Howk (in Caldbeck), 11
Howk Ghyll, near Caldbeck, 11
Howtown, *74*
Hughes, Ted, 198
Hurd, Hugh, 'the Troutbeck Giant', 106–7
Hutchinson, William, 198
  Excursions to the Lakes, 147
  History and Antiquities of Cumberland (1794), *147*
  History of the County of Cumberland (1794), 120–21
Hutton Tower, 153

Ibbetson, Julius Caesar, 194–5
  'Ambleside, The Market Place', 195, *195*
  'Castle Crag, Borrowdale', *141*, 195
  'The Painter's Home', *194*
  'Ullswater from Gowbarrow', 195
ice ages, 16–18
Ill Bell ridge, above Troutbeck, *47*
Inglewood Forest, 58, 119

244

Ireby, 94, 95–6, 236
  Sun Inn at, 222
Ireby Fair, 96, *96*, *97*, 98–9, *98*, *99*,
  101–2, 104
Iron Age, 32, 44, *44*, 45, *46*
Irt, River, 14
Irthington, 57
Irton Cross, 52, *53*

James I, King, 60, 84, 111
Jeffery, Thomas, maps of, 138, *138*,
  143
Jones, Owen Glynne, 173, *174*,
  175–7

Keats, John, 222, *223*
  Hyperion, 156
Kendal, 18, 28, 52, 57
  Abbot Hall museum, 167, 178
  castles, 57
  market, 57
  school of painters, 185
  woollen industry, 76
Kentigern, St (or St Mungo), 51
Kentmere:
  Swaledale sheep, *159*
  Viking spearhead from, *54*
Kern Knotts Crack on Great Gable,
  10
Keswick, 21, 28, 29, 141, 235
  grammar school, 76
  lead pencils, 85
  sports, 117
  tourism, 154
  Vale of, 14, 198
Killington, 53
Kirkby Lonsdale grammar school, 76
Kirkby Stephen grammar school, 76
Kirkstile slates, 7
Knut, King, 56

Lady Ern the Giant legend, 126
Lake Poets, 218; *see also* Coleridge;
  Southey; Wordsworth
Lamb, Charles, 222
land clearances, 21, 32
Langdales, 8, 13, 236
  stone axes from, *33*
  see also Great Langdale; Little
    Langdale
Langdale Pikes, *9*, *19*, *36*, *182*
Langdale Rhyolites, 9
language (local dialect), 52–3, 54, 62,
  63–6, 71–3

place names, 52–3
  wrestling terms, 107–8
  writers using dialect, 225–7
Lanercost monastery, 59
lead, lead quarrying, 27, 32, 85
Lear, Edward, 182, *183*
legends, *55*, 118–26, 147; *see also*
  traditions
Lely, Sir Peter, 185
Liddel, 57
Lingmoor Fell, *36*
Little Langdale, *208*
  clipping sheep in, *82*
Lodore Falls, *179*, 181, *219*
  Southey's poem about, 218
Long Meg and her Daughters, 34
Lord's Rake, Scafell Crag, *15*
Lorton, 14, 59, 236
Low Wood Inn, 153
Loweswater, 7, 59
Lowick, *110*

map(s), 57, *57*, 144–6, *147*, 150, *151*
Martineau, Harriet, 129, *154*, 155,
  157, 222
Maryport, 11, 45, *45*, 86, 234
Mayburgh, 32
Mellbreak, 7
Mesolithic man, 31
Millom, 233
mining, minerals, 27, 85–6, 91–4
  Brandlehow Mine, *91*
  sixteenth-century techniques, *86*
Monk's Bridge, 26
Morecambe, 14, 233
Mosser slates, 7
Muncaster Castle, 14, 60
  'Luck' of, 127
Muncaster Cross, 54
Muncaster Hall, 124
Mungo, St, *see* Kentigern, St
Mungrisdale, 51
Musgrave, 130

Napes Needle, *173*, 174
National Park, 28, 29
  Brockhole, Windermere, *165*
National Trust, founding of, 163, 165
Neolithic man, 19, 31–2
New Red Sandstone, 12, *70*
Newlands Valley, 85, 145
Nibthwaite, *see* High Nibthwaite
Nicholson, Norman, *40*, 230, 233
  'The Sea to the West', 230–31

Normans, 50, 56–60, 61, 84
Norsemen, 53–6, 62, 75, 83–4, 106
North, Christopher, 108, 222
Northumbria, 51–2
Nutter family of painters, 193

Ogilby map, 136
Old Man of Coniston, The, *28*
Old Penrith, 48
Ordnance Survey map, 143
Ordovician era, 10
Ormside bowl, *53*
Orton Scar, Viking silver brooch
   from, *55*
Otley, Jonathan, *6*

painters and engravers, 178–96
   engravers, 187–91
   families of painters, 193
   Kendal school, 185
   see also photographers
Papcastle, 48
Pasche Egg Hill, 128–9
Peel, John, 58
   Graves's song about, 113–14, *114*
   oil painting by J. H. Smith, *161*
pele towers, 60, *60*, *159*, *205*
Pennington Church, tympanum stone
   from, *63*
Penrith, 11, 12, 28
   Castle, *59*
   'the Giant's Grave' in churchyard,
      52
   grammar school, 75
   market, 57
Penrith Sandstone, 34
Petillius Ceriales, 47
photographers, photographs, 178,
      179, 191, 193
   rock-climbing, *172*, 173–4
   see also painters
Pike of Blisco, *8*
Pike of Stickle, 19–20, 32
   stone axe factory, *19*, 20
Pillar mountain, *23*
Pillar Rock, ascent of, 173
Place Fell, *162*
place-names, 53;
   see also language
Plumland, 52
Pocklington, Joseph, 150
   follies on Derwent Isle, *151*

Potter, Beatrix, *161*, 193, 227
   journals of, 227–9
   picture-letter of, *229*
Priory Hotel, Windermere, *156*
Pulpit Rock, *15*
Pyne, J. B., *88*, 191

Raiset Pike, 32
Ransome, Arthur, 193–4, 229
Ranulph de Meschines, Earl of
   Chester, 57, 59
Ravenglass, 14, 171, *210*
   bath-house, 49, *49*
   Roman fort, 48
Rawnsley, Canon H. D., 132, 158,
      163, *163*, 224–5
Red Tarn, *17*
Riggindale, *157*
Risehow, Maryport, 45, *45*
Robinson, Mary, 'the Beauty of
   Buttermere', *125*, 126
Romans, 45, 46–50, 51, *51*, *68*, 85, 106
Romney, George, 185
Rosthwaite, 8, 54
Roughton Gill, 2
Round House, Belle Isle, *152*, 153
Rowlandson, Thomas, *89*, 190, *192*
Ruskin, John, 6, 157–8, *158*, 182, 184,
      193, 222
   'Thirlmere' by, 182, *183*
Rydal Mount (Wordsworth's home),
      217
Rydal Old Hall, 153
Rydal Water, 3, 14, 16, 194, 235

Saddleback, *see* Blencathra
St Anthony's Chapel, Cartmel Fell,
      204
St Bees, 12, 31, 50, 52
   grammar school, 76
   monastery, 59
St John's in the Vale, 14, 120
   Castle Rocks, 56, 120, *121*
St Mary of Furness Abbey, 59, *70*, 75,
      87, 124
Sawrey, Beatrix Potter's home at, 229
Saxton, Christopher, Map of (1574–
      1577), 136, *136*
Scafell, 12, 13, 14, 16, 22, 29, 32, 49,
      51, 54, *135*, 161–2, 179
   Broad Stand, *171*
   Coleridge's descent of, 169–70
Scafell Crag, *15*

Scale Force, *149*
Scaleby Castle, near Carlisle, 189
Schwitters, Kurt, 184
  'Bridge House, Ambleside' by, *142*,
    184
Scott, Sir Walter, 118, 125
  'The Bridal of Trierman', 120, *121*
Seathwaite, 236
Seaton, 54
Sellafield, Bronze Age circle and
  atomic plant at, *238*; *see also*
  Windscale
Septimus Severus, 48
Shap, 11, 59
  granite, 16, 27
  monastery, 59
sheep farming, 21, 30, 75, *78, 79, 80*,
  82
shepherd's crooks and sticks, *101, 103*
Shelley, Percy Bysshe, 222
Silurian Age, 10–11
silver, 27, 32, 55, 85
Sizergh Castle, *205*
Skiddaw, 6, 7, 12, 22, *38–9*, 94, 144,
  145, *190, 209*
Skiddaw Forest, 58
Skiddaw Slates, 7, 9
slate, 7
  quarrying, 27, 85, *203, 208*
Sleddale Forest, 58
Smith, John 'Warwick', 189–90
  'Ferry on Windermere', 190
Smith, Thomas, of Derby, 178, 187–8,
  190
  'View of Derwentwater', 188, *189*
  'View of Windermere', 187–8, *188*
Soulby Fell, 124
Sour Milk Gill, 16
Souther Fell, the Phantoms of
  (legend), 120–21, 147
Southey, Robert, 217, *217*
  Lodore Falls poem, 218
  Wordsworth's friendship with, 217
Speed Map, 136
sports, 105–17
  cock-fighting, 111–12
  fell running, 114, *116*, 117
  hound trailing, 105, 109–11, 112
  hunting, 58, 105, 112–14
  rock climbing, 169–74, 175–7
  skiing, *168*
  wrestling, 105–9
Stainton, 111

'Statesmen' (independent farmers),
  83–5
Steadman, George, of Asby, *106*, 107,
  107
Steele, Christopher 'the Count', 185
Stell, John, *87*
Stockley Bridge, 26
stone circles, 34, 43, 44, 124
stone quarrying, 85
Stott Park bobbin mill, Finsthwaite,
  92–3
Striding Edge, 16, *17*, 29, 125
Sty Head Garnetiferous series, 9
Sty Head track, *135*
Sunbiggin Tarn, 32
Swinside Circle, 34, *43*
Swirral Edge, 16

Thirlmere, *88*, 158, *164*, 182, *183*
Thornthwaite Forest, 58
threshing:
  hand, 77
  steam machine, *79*
Throstle Garth bridge, 26
Thurston Water *see* Coniston Water
Tilli fort, near Coniston, 56
tools and weapons, *19*, 20, *32–3, 33*,
  43, 44, *54*
tourism, 29, 61, 133–7, 146, 147, 150
Towne, Francis, 'Grasmere by the
  Road', *141*
Town End, Troutbeck, *83*, 84
traditions and superstitions, 126–32
  calendar lore, 128–9
  'Lucks', 127–8
  rum butter for lying-in, 130–32
  weddings and funerals, 129–30
  see also legends
Troutbeck, *47*, 83, 84, 95
  'passing bell', 130
Tucker family of painters, 193
Turner, J. M. W., 179–80, 182, 186
  'Morning Amongst the Coniston
    Fells', *139*, 179–80
  Scafell study, 179
  'Torrent in Spate, Coniston', 180

Uldale, 102, 126, 236
Ullswater, 14, 54, *74, 90, 166, 192*, 195
  daffodils at Gowbarrow Park, 67
  fox-hunting, 113
  Joseph Wright's painting of, *90*,
    181–2

247

Ulverston, 33, 234
upper Eskdale, *13*
Urswick, 130, 235

Vikings (Norsemen), 50, 53–6, 62
volcanic rocks, 8–10

Waberthwaite Cross, 52
Wall End, Great Langdale, 27
Walla Crag, 124
Walney, Isle of, 31, 234
Walpole, Hugh, *231*
   The Herries Chronicle, 230
Warcop, 130
Warton Crag, 32
Wasdale, 14, 129
   chapel, 76
   Shepherd's Meet, 236
Wasdale Head, *24*
   farmstead, *76*
   packhorse bridge, 26
   rock-climbing at, 171–3
   village school, *71*
Wast Water, 14, 18, *35*
   Screes, 18, *40*
Watendlath, 230
West, Thomas, 150, 198
   Guide to the Lakes, 145, 150
Wetheral monastery, 59
Whicham, 53
Whitbarrow Scar, *41*
Whitehaven, 11, 87–8, 185, 234
Wigton, 53, 57, 95
   Horse Fair, 236
William of Gospatrick, 106
Wilson, Professor John
   ('Christopher North'), 154, *154*
Winandermere, Wenandremere, *see*
   Windermere
Windermere, 13, 14, 16, 57, 59, 75,
   133–4, 195
   Belle Isle on, *152*, 153, *153*, 235
   Brockhole, 165, *165*
   nineteenth-century mansions in
     area, 153
   paintings and prints of, *88*, 187–8,
     188, 190, *196*

Priory Hotel, *156*
tourism, 154
town, 154
Wray Castle, *155*
Windscale atomic energy station, 91,
   see also Sellafield
Witherslack, Viking sword from, *54*
Wolstey Hall, near Silloth, 45
woollen industry, 75, 76, 84
Wordsworth, Dorothy, 3, *67*, 132,
   155, 197, 202, 211, *212–213*, 214,
   215, 220
   Crosthwaite's portrait of, 194
   journals of, 211, *212*–13, 214, 227
Wordsworth, John, 198, 203
Wordsworth, Mary (*née* Hutchinson),
   215, 216
Wordsworth, William, 22, 49, 118,
   125–6, 150, 152, *152*, 155, 157,
   161, 190, 194, 197, 198, 199–202,
   211–17, 220–22, 231–2, 236
   'Daffodils', 211–15
   De Quincey's account of first
     meeting with, 220, 222
   Guide to the Lakes, 13–16, 190
   'Immortality Ode', 211
   'Lucy poems', 215–16
   'Michael', 126, 215
   preface to *Lyrical Ballads*, 202
   Prelude, The, 200, 202, 211
   'The Recluse', *237*
   Southey's friendship with, 217–18
   'Tintern Abbey', 201–2
Workington, 53, 86, 234
   Cross, 52
   'Luck' of, 127
Wray Castle, Windermere, *155*
Wright of Derby, Joseph, 181–2
   'Ullswater', *90*, 181–2
writers, 197–202, 211–18, 222
Wrynose, 48
Wythburn, 14, 76, *88*
Wythop Hall, 60

Yewtree Farm and 'spinning gallery',
   159
Young, Arthur, 76–7, 144

Internet links

Throughout this book, we have suggested interesting Web sites where you can find out more about mummies and pyramids. To visit the sites, go to the **Usborne Quicklinks Web site** at **www.usborne-quicklinks.com** and type the keywords "discovery mummies". There you will find links to click on to take you to all the sites. Here are some of the things you can do on the recommended sites:

- Take a virtual tour inside the passages of the Great Pyramid at Giza.

- Watch a mummy's face being reconstructed with computer technology.

- Travel through the Egyptian Underworld and defend yourself with magic spells.

- See photographs of the treasures from Tutankhamun's tomb.

Internet safety

When using the Internet, please make sure you follow these guidelines:

- Ask your parent's or guardian's permission before you connect to the Internet.

- If you write a message in a Web site guest book or on a Web site message board, do not include any personal information, such as your full name, address or telephone number, and ask an adult before you give your e-mail address.

- If a Web site asks you to log in or register by typing your name or e-mail address, ask the permission of an adult first.

- If you receive an e-mail from someone you don't know, tell an adult and do not reply to the e-mail.

- Never arrange to meet anyone you have talked to on the Internet.

Site availability

The links in **Usborne Quicklinks** are regularly reviewed and updated, but occasionally you may get a message saying that a site is unavailable. This might be temporary, so try again later, or even the next day.

If any of the sites close down, we will, if possible, replace them with suitable alternatives, so you will always find an up-to-date list of sites in **Usborne Quicklinks**.

Downloadable pictures

Pictures in this book marked with a ★ symbol can be downloaded from **Usborne Quicklinks** for your own personal use — for example, to illustrate a homework report or project. The pictures are the copyright of Usborne Publishing and may not be used for any commercial or profit-related purpose. To download a picture, go to **Usborne Quicklinks** and follow the instructions there.

Note for parents and guardians

The Web sites described in this book are regularly reviewed and the links in **Usborne Quicklinks** are updated. However, the content of a Web site may change at any time and Usborne Publishing is not responsible for the content of any Web site other than its own.

We recommend that children are supervised while on the Internet, that they do not use Internet Chat Rooms, and that you use Internet filtering software to block unsuitable material. Please ensure that your children read and follow the safety guidelines printed on the left. For more information, see the **Net Help** area on the **Usborne Quicklinks Web site**.

Computer not essential

If you don't have access to the Internet, don't worry. This book is a complete, superb, self-contained reference book on its own.

Mummies & Pyramids

Sam Taplin

Designed by Stephanie Jones

Illustrated by John Woodcock
Additional illustrations by Ian Jackson
Consultant: Dr. Anne Millard
Series editor: Gillian Doherty

Contents

4   Mummies and pyramids

6   The afterlife

8   Making mummies

10   Coffins and cases

12   Funerals and grave goods

14   Houses of eternity

16   The pyramid builders

18   Pyramid power

20   Tomb raiders

22   Mummy mania

24   The tomb of Tutankhamun

26   Tutankhamun fever

28   Beastly bodies

30   Myths and movies

32   Fakes and frauds

34   Unwrapping a mummy

36   The mummy speaks

38   Mummies around the world

40   Natural mummies

42   Unsolved mysteries

44   An ongoing quest

46   Using the Internet

47   Index

48   Acknowledgements

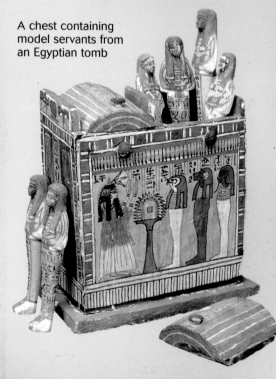

A chest containing model servants from an Egyptian tomb

Internet links

Look for the Internet links boxes throughout this book. They contain descriptions of Web sites where you can find out more about mummies and pyramids. For links to these Web sites, go to **www.usborne-quicklinks.com** and type the keywords "discovery mummies".

★ Next to some of the pictures in the book you will see a symbol like this. Wherever you see one of these symbols, it means that you can download the picture from the **Usborne Quicklinks Web site**. For more information on using the Internet, and downloading Usborne pictures, see inside the front cover and page 46.

Cover: A statue of the pharaoh Ramesses II
Title page: The pyramids at Giza
Left: The funeral mask of Tutankhamun

Mummies and pyramids

Ancient Egypt was a long, narrow country along the River Nile. By 5,000 years ago, the Egyptians had created one of the world's first great civilizations. But they are particularly famous for two reasons: they preserved dead people as mummies, and they built huge pyramids as tombs.

Internet links

For a link to a Web site where you can find out more about everyday life for rich people and poor people in ancient Egypt, go to **www.usborne-quicklinks.com**

What is a mummy?

A mummy is a preserved dead body. Normally, the body of a person or animal starts to decay soon after death, but mummies don't rot like this. Mummification (making mummies) was very important to the ancient Egyptians. They believed that dead people continued living in another world, and they thought that the spirit needed the body in order to enjoy the next world.

As well as people, the Egyptians also made dead animals into mummies. This is the mummy of a calf.

This photograph shows the famous pyramids at Giza, in Egypt.

Why "mummies"?

People once thought that the Egyptians used a sticky, black substance called bitumen to preserve their dead. The Arabic word for bitumen is *mummiya*, and from this we get the word "mummy".

Pyramid tombs

The pyramids were built as tombs for the mummies of some Egyptian kings, or pharaohs. No one had ever made such enormous buildings before, and the Great Pyramid at Giza became one of the legendary wonders of the ancient world.

Fact: The Great Pyramid at Giza contains more than two million massively heavy blocks of stone.

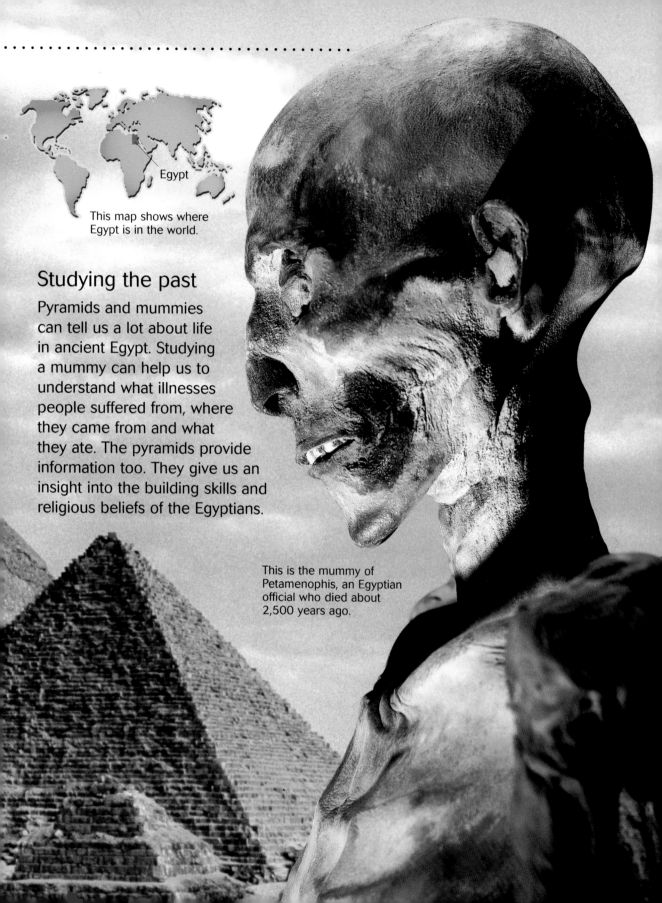

This map shows where Egypt is in the world.

Studying the past

Pyramids and mummies can tell us a lot about life in ancient Egypt. Studying a mummy can help us to understand what illnesses people suffered from, where they came from and what they ate. The pyramids provide information too. They give us an insight into the building skills and religious beliefs of the Egyptians.

This is the mummy of Petamenophis, an Egyptian official who died about 2,500 years ago.

The afterlife

The Egyptians believed in an afterlife. This means a world beyond this one where people go when they die. Being made into a mummy and buried in a tomb wasn't the end of life, but the start of the greatest adventure of all.

The Field of Reeds

The Egyptians imagined a heaven ruled by a god called Osiris. The kingdom of Osiris was a beautiful sunny land called the Field of Reeds. There, surrounded by golden wheat and fruit trees, people ate, drank and were happy all day long.

The crops in the Field of Reeds were huge, but harvesting them was always easy. ★

A terrifying journey

Reaching the kingdom of Osiris wasn't easy. First, you had to survive a long and dangerous journey through the murky passages of the Underworld. Blocking your path were evil spirits, deadly snakes and lakes of fire.

A ferryman took you across the River of Death.

Fire-breathing snakes ★ guarded the way.

This tomb painting shows Osiris, ruler of the Underworld.

Magic charms like this heart amulet were buried with mummies, to help people survive the Underworld.

Weighing the heart

The greatest test came at the end. Your heart was weighed against a feather, and your life was judged by Osiris. If your heart was heavy with wickedness, it would be gobbled up by a monster. But people who had lived a good life could enter the Field of Reeds.

The Book of the Dead

While they were alive, Egyptians learned magic spells to help them face the perils of the Underworld. About 3,500 years ago, these spells were collected and written down in a book known as the Book of the Dead. Wealthy people were buried with a copy of this book, hoping that the spells inside it would protect them on their journey through the Underworld.

This scene from the Book of the Dead shows a person's heart being weighed.

Anubis, god of embalming, held the dead person's hand.

Ammit the 'devourer', who ate the hearts of wicked people

Osiris sat on his throne and judged the dead person.

Internet links

For a link to a Web site where you can use magic spells to defend yourself as you take a journey through the Egyptian Underworld, go to **www.usborne-quicklinks.com**

The royal afterlife

The powerful pharaohs were the only ones who had a different afterlife. Instead of going to the Field of Reeds, they became gods and floated up to join the other gods in the sky.

Fact: The Egyptians had hundreds of gods and goddesses, who looked after everything from baking bread to fighting battles.

Making mummies

The ancient Egyptians were the most skilled and dedicated mummy-makers in history. Preserving the dead was important to their culture, and they invented a complicated way of doing it.

Canopic jars, decorated with the heads of gods, were used to store the mummy's internal organs. The jars were buried inside the mummy's tomb.

Internet links

For a link to a Web site where you can click on different parts of a mummy to find out more about how mummies were made, go to **www.usborne-quicklinks.com**

Although they are thin and dried out, many mummies are still very well preserved beneath the bandages. This is the pharaoh Ramesses II.

A grisly job

It took the Egyptians 70 days to mummify, or embalm, a body, and the embalmers had to cope with blood, guts and awful smells. First, they pushed a sharp rod up through the nose and into the brain. The brain was broken up and pulled out through the nose.

A hole was made in the body, and the embalmers pulled out all the internal organs except for the heart.

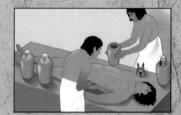

The hole was stuffed with linen and spices, then the body was left under a salt called natron to dry it out.

After 40 days, the body was carefully wrapped in linen bandages. Priests said spells while the body was wrapped.

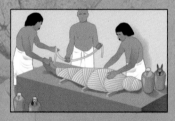

★

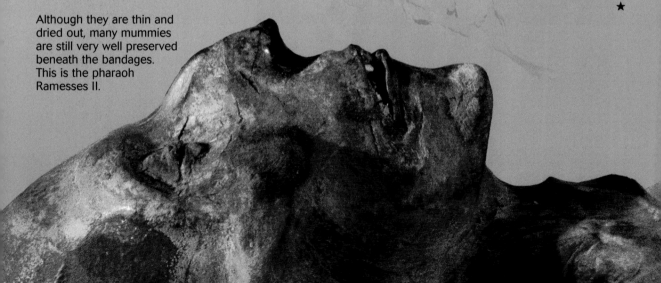

Magnificent masks

When the mummy was finished, a mask was placed over the bandaged face, so that the person could be recognized in the afterlife. Some masks showed a highly realistic portrait of the dead person.

The mummy industry

Lots of people were needed to prepare and bury mummies. There were coffin-makers and tomb-builders, and some people worked as professional mourners. They wailed and screamed at funerals, to show how much the dead person was missed.

This mask was made for a rich woman who died about 2,500 years ago.

Coffins and cases

When the Egyptians had finished making a mummy, they placed it in a coffin to give it extra protection. The earliest coffins were simple cases made from reeds or wood, but later ones were beautifully decorated.

Internet links

For a link to a Web site with a clickable coffin which you can use to find out the meaning behind the paintings on Egyptian coffins, go to **www.usborne-quicklinks.com**

Decorated coffins

About 4,000 years ago, the Egyptians started painting coffins with pictures of objects the dead person might need in the afterlife. The inside was just as carefully decorated as the outside.

Nests of coffins

Early coffins were a simple rectangular shape, but later ones were shaped like people. The mummies of royals and wealthy Egyptians were given special protection by being placed in a nest of two or three human-shaped coffins, one inside the other. The coffins of a pharaoh might be solid gold or silver.

Here you can see the lavishly decorated inside of a human-shaped coffin.

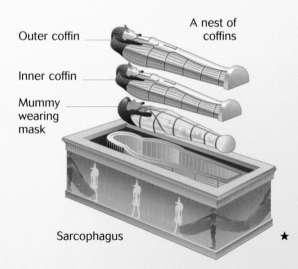

A nest of coffins

Outer coffin

Inner coffin

Mummy wearing mask

Sarcophagus ★

Sealed in stone

The outermost coffin of a pharaoh was a big stone box called a sarcophagus. About 4,500 years ago, these heavy rectangular boxes were left undecorated, or were carved with a picture of a royal palace.

Later, they were carved with pictures of four goddesses, one guarding each corner. By 2,500 years ago, a completely different human-shaped sarcophagus had become fashionable.

This beautifully carved sarcophagus was made for Sasobek, an Egyptian minister who died around 2,500 years ago.

From around 1,300 years ago, a portrait of the dead person was left in their coffin. This portrait shows a wealthy woman wearing earrings and a necklace.

Funerals and grave goods

Once an Egyptian mummy was inside its coffin, it was taken to its tomb in a solemn funeral procession. Then, it was buried along with many objects, known as grave goods. These were meant to help the dead person in the afterlife.

Internet links

For a link to a Web site where you can see photographs of Egyptian grave goods including furniture, model servants and gold treasures, go to **www.usborne-quicklinks.com**

Journey to the tomb

The coffin was placed on a wooden boat, which was pulled along on a sled by oxen and men. Priests walked ahead, saying prayers and burning sweet-smelling incense. Servants followed, carrying the grave goods for the tomb, while mourners wailed in distress. Later, there was a feast for family and friends, and offerings were made to the dead person's spirit.

★ This glass perfume-holder was buried in an Egyptian tomb.

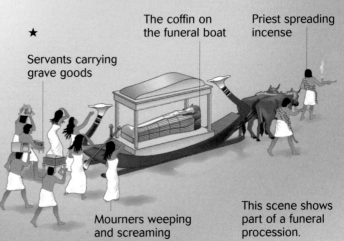

★ Servants carrying grave goods

The coffin on the funeral boat

Priest spreading incense

Mourners weeping and screaming

This scene shows part of a funeral procession.

Ready for the afterlife

Dead people were expected to continue leading a normal life. So they were buried with an amazing variety of different objects to keep them comfortable and entertained. There were beds, clothes, musical instruments, and even board games.

Wealthy Egyptians were buried with lots of precious jewels and ornaments, such as this golden earring.

Servants and feasts

Dead people were provided with small model servants to look after them, prepare food, keep animals and grow crops in the next world. In later times, people were buried with 365 servants, one for each day of the year.

Real food, such as fruit and meat, was left in the tomb as well. Relatives were supposed to leave more food for the dead person every day, but people mainly did this on important festivals.

The Opening of the Mouth

Before the mummy was sealed inside its burial chamber, a priest performed a ritual known as the Opening of the Mouth. He touched the mummy's ears, eyes and mouth with sacred objects. This was to allow the dead person to hear, see and speak in the next world.

This model servant from an Egyptian tomb is bringing bread for the dead person.

This scene shows priests performing the Opening of the Mouth ceremony.

Houses of eternity

Early Egyptians buried people in holes in the desert, and poor people were buried in this way throughout Egyptian civilization. But pharaohs and nobles were laid to rest in tombs that would last forever and show the world their glory.

Internet links

For a link to a Web site where you can see great photos of the first step pyramid and find out more about how it was built, go to **www.usborne-quicklinks.com**

Mastabas

The first royal tombs were called mastabas. These were low, rectangular mud-brick buildings, with a burial chamber built beneath them.

Statue of the dead noble

A mastaba

Ground level

Mourners brought offerings for the dead.

Underground burial chamber held coffin and grave goods.

★ Passage to burial chamber was blocked with rubble.

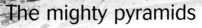

This photograph shows the first step pyramid as it looks today.

The mighty pyramids

Around 4,500 years ago, an architect called Imhotep made a new kind of tomb for the pharaoh Zoser. He built several stone mastabas on top of each other, each one slightly smaller than the last. This made an impressive shape, known as a step pyramid. Soon, all kings were buried inside towering pyramids.

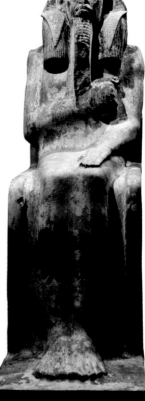

A statue of the pharaoh Zoser

This is part of the rock-cut tomb of Nefertari, wife of the pharaoh Ramesses II. Rock-cut tombs were lavishly painted on the inside.

Royal tombs were decorated with paintings of the gods. This is Re-Harakhti, the sun god.

The Valley of the Kings

Pyramids were so spectacular that robbers couldn't resist breaking in and stealing the treasures. About 3,500 years ago, a cunning pharaoh called Tuthmosis I came up with a solution. His tomb was cut deep into the rock of a hidden valley, now known as the Valley of the Kings. This idea caught on, and soon all pharaohs and their wives were buried in secret rock-cut tombs.

Persistent pyramids

Although pharaohs were no longer buried in pyramids, the pyramid shape remained very important to the Egyptians. Some people had miniature pyramids built over their tombs.

Pyramids also made a comeback in the Kingdom of Kush, a part of Egypt which became independent about 2,700 years ago. The people of Kush copied the Egyptian way of life, and the kings built pyramids which are still standing today.

 Fact: The Valley of the Kings was said to be protected from robbers by a serpent goddess called Meretseger.

15

The pyramid builders

The pyramids were miracles of architecture and organization. Without cranes, drills or machines of any kind, the Egyptians created some of the largest stone buildings ever made.

Internet links

For a link to a Web site where you can take a guided photo tour around the outside and inside of the Bent Pyramid, go to **www.usborne-quicklinks.com**

Early experiments

When the Egyptians first tried to make a pyramid with straight sides instead of steps, they made the sides too steep. They tried to correct this by making them less steep at the top, but this left the pyramid looking a little strange. It became known as the Bent Pyramid.

This photograph shows the Bent Pyramid as it looks today.

A massive task

After that, the Egyptians became masters at building pyramids. For 800 years, these towering tombs sprung up in Egypt. They were built with sheer muscle power and dedication, and making a large one might require as many as 20,000 workmen.

The pyramid still has traces of the white stone that once covered the whole building.

Stage by stage

Building a pyramid was an incredibly complicated job, and the work was done slowly and carefully, in many different stages. For the biggest pyramids, the whole process could take over 20 years to complete. A great deal of work had to be done before the first stone block could be set in place.

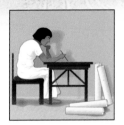

An architect made plans and built models to show to the pharaoh.

Large blocks of stone were carved from quarries with mallets and chisels.

Fact: About ninety pyramids were built throughout Egypt, and most of these are still standing.

Willing workers

People used to think the pyramids were built by slaves who were treated harshly, but the workers were actually free men. They were paid by the pharaoh, and they were proud to be part of such an amazing achievement.

As well as the builders, a massive number of other people were needed to provide all the stone, feed the workers and transport the blocks from the quarry to the building site. This was such a huge effort of organization that building the pyramids helped to transform Egypt into a powerful and efficient country.

Ancient Egyptian tools were very basic compared to modern ones. Most of them were made of wood, with blades made of stone or soft metal, like copper.

Workmen dragged the blocks to boats, which took them down the river to the pyramid site.

All the sand was removed from the site, and the rock was flattened so it would support the building.

As the pyramid grew, the workmen hauled the blocks up huge ramps studded with wooden rollers.

The ramps were gradually removed, and a layer of gleaming polished stone was added.

★

An adze like this was used for shaping the wooden rollers on the pyramid ramps.

Stone balls like this were used to shape hard rocks.

Chisels were useful for delicately shaping wood.

Mallets and chisels were used to carve and shape stone blocks from the quarry.

Pyramid power

The pyramids were far more than just spectacular buildings. They were deeply influenced by Egyptian religion, and were designed to send the dead king to join his fellow gods in heaven.

An Egyptian star chart showing each constellation in the shape of a god or an animal

Stepladders to the stars

The pyramids had many different meanings for the Egyptians. Early kings believed they would join particular constellations (groups of stars) in the afterlife. Texts written on later pyramids describe step pyramids as stepladders to the stars.

Inside the burial chamber of the Great Pyramid at Giza are two narrow vents pointing upward through the rock. These seem to point directly at constellations that were important in Egyptian religion. The vents may have been intended to launch the pharaoh's soul up to the gods.

Sunbeams made of stone

By about 2,500 years ago, the sun god Re had become very important. Pyramids were now thought of as huge ramps, or sunbeams made of stone. The dead king's soul would climb up these ramps and meet Re in the sky.

This picture shows Re, the sun god, making his daily journey across the sky.

Here you can see the pyramids at Giza, the biggest and most famous in Egypt.

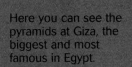

Fact: Temples were built on the eastern side of the pyramids, because this was the direction of the rising sun and rebirth.

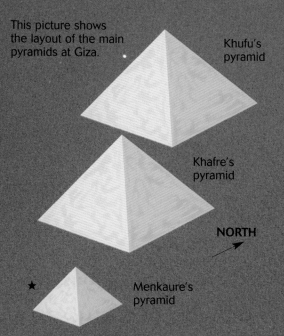

This picture shows the layout of the main pyramids at Giza.

Khufu's pyramid

Khafre's pyramid

NORTH

Menkaure's pyramid

The Giza pyramids are lined up so that their four sides face north, south, east and west. Experts think that the builders used the stars to position them so precisely.

Internet links

For a link to a Web site where you can crawl through the mysterious passageways deep inside the Great Pyramid, go to www.usborne-quicklinks.com

The city of the dead

Today, we think of the pyramids standing alone in the empty desert, but things were very different in ancient times. Next to each pyramid was a temple where priests presented offerings to the dead king every day.

There were also smaller pyramids where queens were buried and mastaba tombs for members of the king's court. The whole group of buildings was called the necropolis, or the city of the dead.

Nearby were palaces and towns where priests and their families lived. These people spent their lives looking after the pyramids and the dead kings.

This small bronze statue shows an Egyptian priest. Priests were powerful in ancient Egypt, and were seen as the servants of the gods.

Out of the waters

The pyramid shape was also connected with an Egyptian belief about the creation of the world. In the beginning, the world was just water, until a mound of earth rose from the depths. Some people thought of the pyramid as a symbol of this mound.

Tomb raiders......................................

Since many Egyptian mummies were buried with fabulous treasures, cemeteries had to be extremely well guarded. But in chaotic periods when the guards were often away, robbers moved in. If caught they faced an awful death, but many still risked their lives to get hold of the pharaohs' riches.

A formidable task

Breaking into a royal rock-cut tomb was far from easy. The doors were sealed shut with stones, then covered with a layer of plaster. The entrance passages were often blocked with huge stone slabs or filled with rubble, so the robbers had to tunnel through to the tomb.

This is part of the tomb of the pharaoh Ramesses IV. Like almost everything else in the Valley of the Kings, his sarcophagus was robbed thousands of years ago.

The robbers made a small tunnel into a tomb, so that they could cover it up afterwards.

They smashed open the chests of treasures and filled their baskets with gold and jewels.

Under cover of night, they loaded their baskets of loot onto donkeys and quickly escaped.

Fact: Some robbers used stolen treasures as part of the grave goods for their own tombs.

Smooth criminals

By about 3,000 years ago, tomb robbing had become a highly organized business. Gangs of raiders had donkeys and boats standing by so they could make a quick getaway. They also prepared secret places to hide all their stolen treasure. Sometimes, tomb guards were paid bribes to keep them quiet.

Magical amulets were left with mummies to protect them, but they didn't discourage robbers.

Modern day robbers

The raiding didn't end with the ancient world. Throughout the centuries, and up to the present day, thieves have continued searching for new tombs to raid. Although tomb robbing is illegal in Egypt, some people are still tempted by the treasures of their ancestors.

Precious objects like this gold necklace have tempted robbers since ancient times.

This statue at Giza is called the Sphinx. A form of the Egyptian sun god, the Sphinx was intended to act as a guardian of the nearby pyramids.

★

Mummy mania

This is the body of Jeremy Bentham, an English philosopher who asked to be mummified when he died.

The head of Bentham's "mummy" is a wax copy, but his real body is preserved beneath his suit.

In the early 1800s, explorers began bringing back Egyptian mummies and tomb treasures to Europe and America. This created a wave of public interest in the ancient Egyptians, and people were gripped by mummy mania.

Mummy hunters

Soon, Egypt was swarming with wealthy collectors who wanted to find their own mummies. Some of these mummy hunters were serious archaeologists who gave their finds to museums, but others just wanted souvenirs to take home.

Public unwrappings

When collectors returned from their travels, they were eager to show off their discoveries. People were fascinated, and mummy viewings became very popular. Some collectors went even further, and actually unwrapped a mummy before specially invited guests. This wasn't always easy, and on one occasion the mummy had to be sawn open.

A 19th-century drawing of a mummy being unwrapped

Fact: Not everyone treasured mummies. Some were even used as fuel in steam engines.

Becoming mummies

Some wealthy people got so carried away that they decided to be made into mummies themselves when they died. Other people asked to be buried with Egyptian-style pyramids and obelisks as gravestones.

This is the Washington Monument in the USA, which was built in the shape of an Egyptian obelisk.

Egyptian styles

During the 1920s, when Tutankhamun's tomb was discovered, the interest in ancient Egypt created a new craze for Egyptian-style furniture, buildings and jewels. For a while, a brooch in the shape of an Egyptian scarab beetle was the height of fashion. Even today, Egyptian style has a powerful influence over designers.

A brooch made in the 1930s, shaped to look like the head of an ancient Egyptian pharaoh

Egyptian architecture remains very popular today. These statues are part of a hotel in Las Vegas, USA.

The tomb of Tutankhamun...............

The most famous Egyptian tomb of all was built for Tutankhamun, the boy king who died when he was not much more than 18 years old.

An early death

Tutankhamun became pharaoh of Egypt around 3,370 years ago, when he was about nine years old. Less than ten years later he was dead, and no one is sure why. Some people have even suggested that he may have been murdered. The young pharaoh was mummified and sealed in a tomb in the Valley of the Kings.

In search of history

Over 3,000 years passed. Most Egyptian royal tombs were ransacked by robbers, leaving only fragments of the treasures which had been buried with the pharaohs. Many experts thought there was nothing left to find. But a few determined archaeologists continued to explore the Valley of the Kings, still dreaming of a discovery.

This wooden portrait bust of Tutankhamun was discovered in his tomb.

Internet links

For a link to a Web site where you can read an exciting account of the discovery of the tomb written by a journalist in 1923, go to **www.usborne-quicklinks.com**

tomb has a carved scarab beetle, an Egyptian symbol of the sun.

"Wonderful things"

With his sponsor, Lord Carnarvon, side, Carter removed a stone from tomb door. By the light of a flicker candle, he peered into the darkne When asked if he could see anythi replied, "Yes, wonderful things!"

The chamber was packed with a d array of statues, chariots, caskets a vases. Gold gleamed everywhere i candlelight. It was some of the mo amazing treasure ever found.

This photograph shows Howard Carter and his assistants opening a shrine inside the tomb.

Tutankha wooden was de with gc and je

An amazing find

In 1922, a British archaeologist named Howard Carter was searching the Valley of the Kings. He had almost given up hope of finding anything new, when beneath the rubble from another tomb he found steps leading down into the rock. He followed them, and eventually came to a plastered wall bearing the seals of Egyptian priests. It was the tomb of Tutankhamun.

Fact: Tutankhamun's tomb was a very small one, so we can only imagine the treasures that once lay in the larger tombs in the Valley of the Kings.

Tutankhamun fever

The discovery of Tutankhamun's tomb thrilled the world. As Carter and Carnarvon removed the treasures, they were surrounded by fascinated onlookers. Hundreds of journalists, photographers and other visitors from across the world flocked to Egypt, hoping for a glimpse of the wonders.

This photograph shows the crowds around the tomb entrance as treasures were removed.

Treasure hoard

Among the objects filling the tomb were statues of gods, painted chests, board games, lamps and necklaces. There was also lots of real food that had been left for the pharaoh. Because there were so many fragile treasures, it took years to remove them all.

Internet links

For a link to a Web site where you can see lots of photographs of the spectacular treasures found in Tutankhamun's tomb, go to www.usborne-quicklinks.com

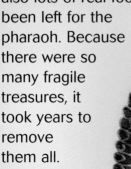

This hawk-shaped pendant was just one of the many treasures found in the tomb.

The moment of truth

Carter soon realized that ancient thieves had broken into the tomb and escaped with a few small items. But no one knew whether the pharaoh's burial chamber, which would contain the most precious treasures of all, had been raided. At last, three years after finding the tomb, Carter was ready to find out.

Meeting the mummy

Inside the burial chamber was a magnificent sarcophagus made of red stone. Within it was a nest of three coffins, the last one made of solid gold. When Carter opened this, he became the first person to see Tutankhamun's mummy in 3,000 years.

Tutankhamun's mummified head

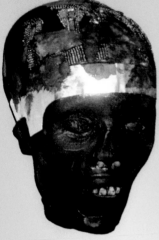

A stunningly beautiful golden mask lay over the face, and more than a hundred amulets and jewels were wrapped up in the bandages. But, sadly, the materials that should have preserved the body had actually damaged it badly.

The golden funeral mask shows a portrait of the young pharaoh.

Beastly bodies

The Egyptians didn't stop at mummifying people. Animals were very important to their religion, and they made them into mummies too.

Sacred beasts

The Egyptians mummified lots of different animals, including cats, crocodiles and baboons. They believed that gods could send their spirit to Earth to enter the bodies of a few special creatures, so it was important to preserve them. For example, Amun, the king of the gods, could appear as a ram or a goose, while a falcon flying overhead might actually be Horus, the sun god.

This is the wall of an Egyptian temple. The ram's head in the middle is a symbol of the god Amun.

Lives of luxury

Animals who were thought to represent gods lived next to the god's temple, and were lovingly cared for. When they died, they were made into mummies and buried with a respectful ceremony. Their coffins were sometimes just as beautifully decorated as human coffins.

This golden coffin was made for an ibis, a sacred Egyptian bird.

Some animals, such as this cat, were wrapped in intricately patterned bandages.

A crocodile mummy

Internet links

For a link to a Web site where you can find out more about different types of animal mummies and how they were made, go to **www.usborne-quicklinks.com**

The Apis bulls

Although many animals were made into mummies, a few were particularly important. The most famous is the Apis bull, who was thought to contain the spirit of the god Ptah.

The Apis bull was always black with white markings.

★

The bull was visited by the worshippers of Ptah, and it was thought that it had the power to predict the future. When it died, it was made into a mummy and buried in a huge stone sarcophagus. Then, a new bull was chosen to be the Apis bull.

Dogs were popular pets in ancient Egypt, and lots of them were mummified.

A huge industry

By about 2,500 years ago, Egyptians thought that every single animal contained part of a god's spirit. Making animal mummies became more and more popular, and thousands of people were employed to do the work. People bought these mummies, then buried them in animal cemeteries, as a way of pleasing the gods. Many millions of animals were mummified in this way.

Fact: In the 19th century, thousands of ancient mummified cats were shipped from Egypt to England, to be ground up and used as fertilizer.

Myths and movies

Mummies and pyramids have always inspired the imagination. Movies about mummies that come to life are very popular, and people enjoy wild stories about magical powers and curses from beyond the grave.

Internet links

For a link to a Web site where you can read the facts about the mysterious "curse" of Tutankhamun and its victims, go to **www.usborne-quicklinks.com**

The curse of Tutankhamun

Lord Carnarvon (on the left) outside the tomb

The most famous myth of all is the curse said to haunt those who disturbed the mummy of the pharaoh Tutankhamun. Lord Carnarvon, who organized the expedition, died less than a year after entering the tomb. At the moment of his death in Cairo, all the lights in the city went out. At the same time, back in England, his beloved dog howled and died. Other people who were said to have visited the tomb also died.

A total invention

Actually, all of these spine-chilling tales are completely untrue. There is no curse written on the wall of Tutankhamun's tomb, and Lord Carnarvon died of nothing more sinister than an infected mosquito bite. Howard Carter, the leader of the expedition and the first man to enter the tomb, lived happily for many more years.

This is one of two life-size statues that guarded Tutankhamun's burial chamber.

The poster for a 1955 movie which took a comic look at the idea of mummies coming back to life

The actor Christopher Lee in the 1959 film, "The Mummy"

Mummies in movies

The story of an angry mummy attacking the explorers who disturb it has been used in lots of movies. The first was made in 1932, not long after Tutankhamun's tomb was opened. People were intrigued by the spooky idea of a living mummy, and many more movies have followed.

Pyramid myths

The pyramids have thrown up just as many bizarre ideas as mummies have. Over the years, people have suggested that pyramids had the power to mummify dead cats left inside them, to preserve food and even to sharpen razor blades. People have also claimed that the Great Pyramid at Giza was built not by the ancient Egyptians but by aliens.

Fakes and frauds

Mummies are big business, and are sold for huge sums of money. This has been true for centuries, and there have always been people who profited by making fake mummies.

Ancient frauds

A dishonest mummy-maker took a bird's head and made a fake body to go with it.

The "mummy" was carefully wrapped with bandages, and looked completely convincing.

Even genuinely ancient mummies aren't always quite what they seem. Animals were important in Egyptian religion, and millions of bird mummies were sold. But when birds were in short supply, some mummy-makers only put part of a bird inside each mummy. The rest was stuffed with rags, feathers and shards of pottery. This became so common that the government eventually had to ban it.

Mummy medicine

In the Middle Ages, a different sort of mummy trade began. Many people believed that powder made by grinding up mummies could cure all kinds of illnesses. For hundreds of years, people swallowed the disgusting stuff to help with sore throats, headaches and even broken bones.

There was a huge demand for the powder, and thousands of mummies were needed to make it all. Some merchants are said to have cashed in by murdering people, drying them in the ★ sand and selling the bodies.

Mummy powder was a highly respected medicine. King Francis I of France used to sprinkle a little of it in his wine every day to keep himself healthy.

A container that was used to hold mummy powder

Internet links

For a link to a Web site where you can compare genuine ancient Egyptian objects with modern fakes, go to
www.usborne-quicklinks.com

Fact: Powdered mummy has even been used to make a type of paint, known as "mummy brown".

Murder mystery

In 2000, a seemingly incredible discovery was made in Pakistan. A perfectly preserved mummy was found, and it appeared to be the body of a Persian princess. It was said to be over 2,500 years old, and made by Egyptian experts. It looked like one of the most amazing finds ever made.

But the truth was far darker. Experts soon realized that the mummy was actually a fake made less than two years earlier. Even worse, the mummified woman may have been murdered to provide the body.

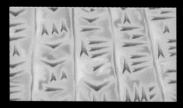 ★

Ancient writing on the mummy's coffin contained mistakes, which made experts suspicious.

When experts examined the body, they discovered that the mummy was a modern fake.

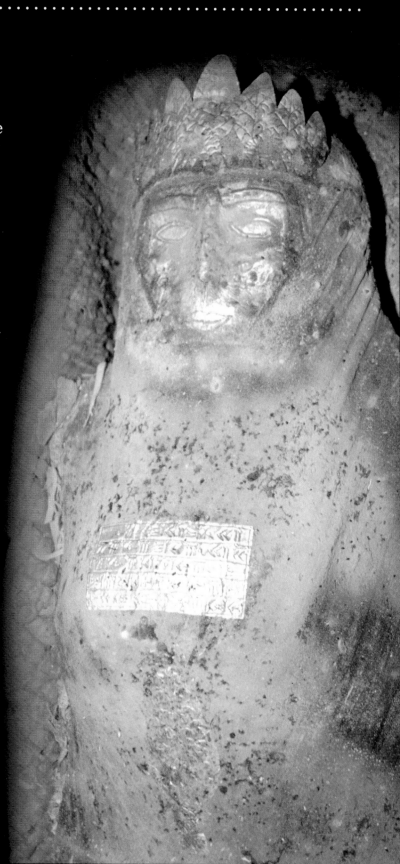

The fake "Persian princess" mummy

Unwrapping a mummy.....

Once, the most common way of examining a mummy was simply to rip the bandages off. But this destroys a lot of evidence, and means the mummy can never be admired whole again. Today, scientists have a range of ways of studying a mummy without harming it.

Scanning the body

Machines used by doctors to look inside people are useful for examining mummies too. X-ray photographs can show us the inside of a mummy's body, as well as any amulets or jewels wrapped with it.

CAT (Computerized Axial Tomography) scanning is even more revealing. A CAT machine makes hundreds of pictures of a mummy's insides. These pictures are combined to form lifelike three-dimensional images which can be rotated.

On this X-ray you can see the outline of a coffin, and the skeleton of the mummy inside it.

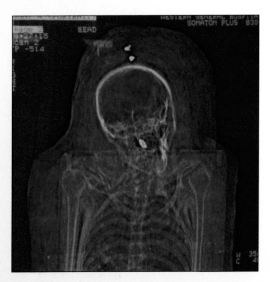

CAT scans of this unwrapped mummy head showed that the empty skull had been stuffed with linen to keep it in shape.

 Fact: X-rays of the pharaoh Ramesses II revealed that his big nose was stuffed with peppercorns to keep it in shape.

A delicate operation

When experts unwrap a mummy today, they do it extremely carefully. A large team of scientists works together, to find out as much as possible. Cloth experts study the bandages, while others look for preserved insects or seeds. Dentists inspect the teeth, which can tell them what kind of diet the person had.

A scientist examining a mummy's foot

Seeing inside

Experts also use a tool called an endoscope to study mummies without damaging them too much. This is a long, very narrow and flexible tube that can be inserted into a body through an opening, such as the nose. The endoscope takes pictures of the mummy's insides, and it can also remove tiny pieces of the body so that these can be studied.

An endoscope can even be inserted through a small hole in a coffin, so that the mummy can be examined without destroying the coffin.

Internet links

For a link to a Web site where you can see how X-rays and CAT scans helped to reveal the hidden secrets of a mummy, go to **www.usborne-quicklinks.com**

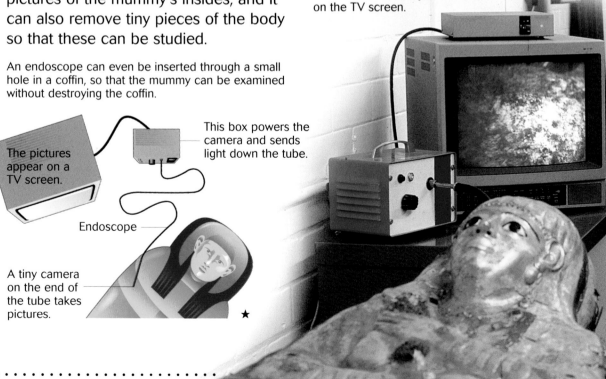

Thanks to an endoscope, scientists can view the mummy in this coffin on the TV screen.

The pictures appear on a TV screen.

This box powers the camera and sends light down the tube.

Endoscope

A tiny camera on the end of the tube takes pictures.

The mummy speaks

As well as looking inside mummies, experts use a variety of ingenious techniques to find out more about them. Preserved bodies can reveal a surprising number of facts about the distant past.

Internet links

For a link to a Web site where you can watch a mummy's face being gradually reconstructed with the help of computer graphics, go to **www.usborne-quicklinks.com**

Meet the relatives

Even tiny fragments of mummies can uncover secrets from thousands of years ago. One way to find out about a mummy is to analyze a chemical called DNA which is found in all living things, and also in things that were once alive.

People who are related to each other have similar DNA, so scientists can use it to trace the family relationships between mummies buried in different tombs.

A model showing the structure of DNA

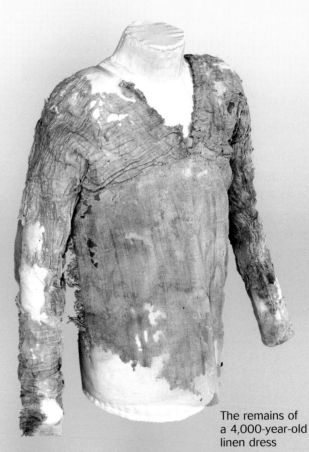

The remains of a 4,000-year-old linen dress

Ancient styles

Sometimes, fragments of ancient cloth or even complete items of clothing are found in tombs. These show us what people wore, and how ancient clothes were made.

Face to face

Although mummies' faces were supposed to be perfectly preserved, only a few of them are. But we can still get a good idea of how they once looked. Using a model of a mummy's skull, a sculptor can reconstruct its face.

First, pegs are used to mark the thickness of the flesh. Then, layers of clay are added, and the shape of the face is built up from the skull. Some mummies were buried with a portrait of the dead person, so by recreating the face we can see how accurate these portraits were.

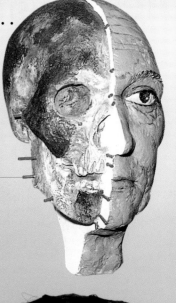

This model shows two different stages in reconstructing a mummy's face.

Pegs to mark the thickness of muscle and skin

Here you can see an ancient mummy portrait, and a finished model of the same woman.

Medical secrets

Studying mummies can also help us to learn what illnesses Egyptians suffered from, what sort of medical care they received, and even whether they had a bad back. All this helps experts to build up a detailed picture of life in ancient times.

Mummies around the world

T he Egyptians are the most famous mummy-makers, but many other ancient peoples also preserved their dead. Here are just a few of them.

South America

China

This map shows the areas of the world where the mummies on these pages were found.

The oldest mummies

Lots of mummies have been found in the mountains and deserts of South America. The Chinchorro people from Chile were making mummies 7,000 years ago. This is 2,000 years before the Egyptians began making theirs.

The Chinchorro had their own way of making mummies. They took the body apart, and replaced the internal organs with clay and feathers. Then, they fastened the body back together with sticks and painted the mummy black.

The head of each Chinchorro mummy was covered with a clay mask.

Internet links

For a link to a Web site where you can see a selection of exciting video clips about different mummies from around the world, go to **www.usborne-quicklinks.com**

Inca mummies

The South American Inca people, who lived in Peru from around 3,000 years ago, made their dead kings into mummies. The kings were dressed in magnificent clothes and paraded through the streets at festivals.

Beautiful failures

In ancient China, people thought that a precious stone called jade had the power to preserve bodies. A few emperors, princes and nobles were buried inside suits made entirely from pieces of jade, sewn together with gold thread.

The only problem was that jade actually had no special powers at all. Although the amazing suits have survived to this day, the bodies of rulers inside them withered away thousands of years ago.

Here you can see a Chinese burial suit made from more than 2,000 pieces of jade.

Fact: The Chinese jade suits were so beautifully made that it took a team of skilled workers about 10 years to make each one.

Natural mummies

ots of mummies are manmade but they can also be formed naturally, when bodies are preserved beneath sand, ice or boggy ground. Natural mummies have been found all over the world, from the ice fields of the Arctic to the baking deserts of Africa.

Bog bodies

Amazingly well preserved mummies can be formed when bodies are left in thick peat bogs. Several mummies found in the bogs of Denmark seem to have been killed as a sacrifice to the gods, then thrown into the bog.

This is Tollund Man, who was left in a bog in Denmark about 2,000 years ago. He had been hanged, and was found with the noose still around his neck.

Internet links

For a link to a Web site where you can find out more about the fascinating story of Ötzi the iceman and see photographs of his weapons, go to **www.usborne-quicklinks.com**

Desert mummies

Many mummies have been created by hot, dry desert sands. In Egypt and South America, bodies buried beneath the sand have been dried out and preserved.

One of the best known desert mummies is an Egyptian man who has been nicknamed Ginger. His ginger hair has survived along with his body for more than 5,000 years.

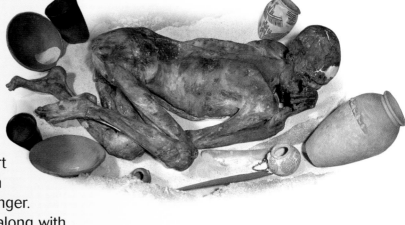

Ginger was buried along with a selection of pots, so that he would have somewhere to store food and drink in the next life.

Beneath the ice

Mummies are also formed when bodies are frozen by ice. The most famous ice mummy was discovered in 1991 by tourists wandering the Alps. It was a man who had died in the mountains over 5,000 years ago.

At first, no one was sure what killed the iceman. Some experts thought he had simply frozen to death in the mountains. But in 2001, experts studied him again and found an arrowhead buried in his shoulder. It now looks as though he was murdered.

Here you can see the iceman, nicknamed Ötzi, soon after he was discovered.

Fact: Many natural mummies still have traces of their last meal in their stomach, which helps to show what ancient people ate.

Unsolved mysteries......................................

Mummies have taught us a massive amount about the ancient world. But some mummies create almost as many questions as they answer, and many secrets remain to be unravelled.

Gruesome ends

In 1975, experts at Manchester University in England examined the mummy of a 14-year-old Egyptian girl. To their surprise, they found that the lower parts of the mummy's legs were missing. No one is sure what lies behind this grisly mystery, but one theory is that the girl had been attacked by a crocodile.

The Manchester mummy was wrapped up to look unharmed. Here you can see its shoes.

Recycled treasures?

A local worker near the entrance of Tutankhamun's tomb soon after it was found

The boy pharaoh Tutankhamun died unexpectedly, but he was buried with amazing treasures. People have always been surprised that so many grave goods could have been made in such a short time. Some experts think that objects were removed from other tombs and reused. So the treasures may not be quite what they seem.

Was this beautiful statuette really made for Tutankhamun?

Tomb 55

In 1907, a new tomb was discovered in the Valley of the Kings. A splendid golden coffin contained a mummy - but whose? Unfortunately, the mummy was handled so roughly by the people who found it that it was reduced to bones.

Panels from a shrine in the tomb were decorated with the name of Queen Tiy, mother of the pharaoh Akhenaten. So the investigators decided the mummy must be hers. However, closer inspection of the bones showed that the mummy was a man - but which man?

This is the coffin found in tomb 55. Rather than helping to clear up the mystery, the coffin only created more questions.

Mystery man

Many experts think that the coffin in tomb 55 was originally made for Kiya, one of Akhenaten's wives. But it seems to have been altered to make the decorations suitable for a pharaoh. Could it be that the bones belong to the legendary Akhenaten himself? We may never know.

A statue of the pharaoh Akhenaten, a strange ruler who tried to change Egypt's religion

Internet links

For a link to a Web site where you can see photographs and plans of the mysterious tomb 55 and read more about it, go to
www.usborne-quicklinks.com

An ongoing quest......

Mummies, pyramids and other tombs have helped us to build up a fascinating picture of ancient Egypt. But our picture is far from complete, and new discoveries are made all the time.

The biggest tomb

In 1987, archaeologists in the Valley of the Kings found the entrance to a tomb. This tomb had been discovered before, but ancient floods had filled it with rubble and people thought it was unimportant.

However, the archaeologists now found that the tomb was far bigger than people had realized. Known as KV5, it is where the sons of the pharaoh Ramesses II were buried. It contains over a hundred chambers, and is the largest rock-cut tomb ever found in Egypt.

Some of the many bodies at the Valley of the Golden Mummies

Valley of the Golden Mummies

In 1993, archaeologists in Egypt made an amazing discovery, when a donkey accidentally stuck its leg through the roof of a chamber. Beneath the sand was a huge cemetery with as many as 10,000 mummies, some of them wearing beautiful masks covered in gold leaf. It will take years to examine all of the mummies, and they may shed new light on ancient Egypt.

Archaeologists examining remains at the Valley of the Golden Mummies

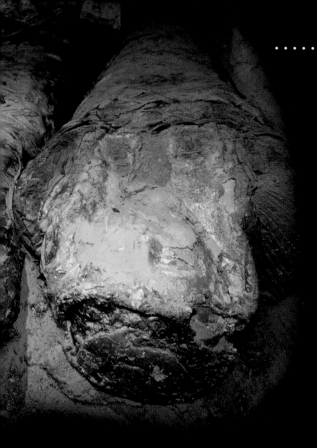

The tomb of Nefertiti

One of the most famous figures in Egyptian history is Queen Nefertiti, wife of the pharaoh Akhenaten. Nefertiti was legendary for her beauty, and has always fascinated historians. But we don't know where she was buried.

Teams of archaeologists still dream of finding her final resting place, and discovering the truth behind the legend.

This famous carved head shows Queen Nefertiti. Finding her mummy might help to show whether she really looked like this.

Internet links

For a link to a Web site where you can explore the chambers inside KV5 and find out the latest news from the tomb, go to
www.usborne-quicklinks.com

Reconstructing pyramids

Many unfinished pyramids and smaller pyramids built for Egyptian queens have been gradually destroyed over the centuries. But experts are now uncovering the remains, and using computer images to show how these magnificent buildings used to look.

A reconstruction showing the ruined pyramids of the queens of the pharaoh Pepy I as they once looked

Fact: Although we have found the tombs of most Egyptian pharaohs, many queens and other royals remain to be discovered.

Using the Internet......................

Most of the Web sites listed in this book can be accessed with a standard home computer and a Web browser (the software that enables you to display information from the Internet).
We recommend:

- A PC with Microsoft® Windows® 98 or later version, or a Macintosh computer with System 9.0 or later, and 64Mb RAM
- A browser such as Microsoft® Internet Explorer 5, or Netscape® Navigator 4.7, or later versions
- Connection to the Internet via a modem (preferably 56Kbps) or a faster digital or cable line
- An account with an Internet Service Provider (ISP)
- A sound card to hear sound files

Extras

Some Web sites need additional programs, called plug-ins, to play sounds, or to show videos, animations or 3-D images. If you go to a site and you do not have the necessary plug-in, a message saying so will come up on the screen. There is usually a button on the site that you can click on to download the plug-in. Alternatively, go to **www.usborne-quicklinks.com** and click on **Net Help**. There you can find links to download plug-ins. Here is a list of plug-ins you might need:

RealPlayer® – lets you play videos and hear sound files.
QuickTime – enables you to view video clips.
Shockwave® – lets you play animations and interactive programs.
Flash™ – lets you play animations.

Help

For general help and advice on using the Internet, go to **Usborne Quicklinks** at **www.usborne-quicklinks.com** and click on **Net Help**. To find out more about how to use your Web browser, click on **Help** at the top of the browser, and then choose **Contents and Index**. You'll find a huge searchable dictionary containing tips on how to find your way around the Internet easily.

Internet safety

Remember to follow the Internet safety guidelines at the front of this book. For more safety information, go to **Usborne Quicklinks** and click on **Net Help**.

Computer viruses

A computer virus is a program that can seriously damage your computer. A virus can get into your computer when you download programs from the Internet, or in an attachment (an extra file) that arrives with an e-mail. We strongly recommend that you buy anti-virus software to protect your computer and that you update the software regularly.

Internet links

For links to Web sites where you can find out more about computer viruses, go to **www.usborne-quicklinks.com** and click on Net Help.

Index

Page numbers in *italic* show where to find pictures.

afterlife 6-7, 9, 11, 12
Akhenaten 43, 45
aliens 31
America 22, 23
Ammit, god 7
amulets *7, 21, 27*, 34
Amun, god 28
animals 4, 12, 13, 18, *28-29*, 32
Anubis, god 7
Apis bulls 29
archaeologists 22, 24, 25, 44-45
architects 14, 16
Arctic 40
bandages 8, 27, 28, 34, 35
Bentham, Jeremy *22*
Bent Pyramid *16*
birds 28, 32
bog mummies *40*
Book of the Dead 7
brooches 23
builders 16-17
burials 12, 13, 14, 15, 28, 29
Cairo 30
Canopic jars *8*
Carnarvon, Lord 25, 26, *30*
Carter, Howard 25, 26, 27, 30
carvings 24, 45
CAT scans 34
cemeteries 20, 29, 44
ceremonies 28
Chile 38
China 39
Chinchorro *38*
chisels *17*
clothes 12, 36
coffins *10-11*, 12, 14, *27*, *28*, *43*

crocodiles 28, 29, 42
curses 30
Denmark 40
desert mummies *41*
DNA 36
earrings 11, 12
embalming *8-9*
endoscopes 35
explorers 22, 31
fake mummies 32-33
festivals 13, 39
Field of Reeds *6*, 7
food 13, 26, 41
Francis I, King of France 32
funerals 9, 12
games 12
Ginger *41*
Giza, Egypt *4-5, 18-19, 21*, 31
gods and goddesses 6, 7, 8, 11, 15, 18, 19, 28, 29
gold 10, 12, 20, 25, 27, 28, 39, 43, 44
grave goods *12-13*, 14, 20, 42
Great Pyramid 4, 18, 31
heaven 6, 18
Horus, god 28
ibises 28, 32
ice mummies *41*
illnesses 5, 32, 37
Imhotep 14
Incas 39
jade suits 39
jewels 20, 23, 25, 27, 34
Kush, Kingdom of 15
KV5 (tomb) 44
Las Vegas, USA 23
mallets *17*
"Manchester girl" 42
masks 9, 10, *27*, *38*, 44
mastabas *14*, 19

medicine 32
Meretseger, goddess 15
Middle Ages 32
mosquitoes 30
mourners 9, 12, 14
movies 30, 31
mummification 4, *8-9*, 29, 38
mummy powder 32
myths 30-31
natron 8
necropolises 19
Nefertari 15
Nefertiti 45
Nile, River 4
Osiris, god *6, 7*
Ötzi the iceman *41*
paintings *10, 11, 15, 37*
Pakistan 33
pendants 26
Pepy I, pharaoh 45
Peru 39
pharaohs 4, 7, 11, 14, 15, 16, 17, 18, 20, 24, 26, 30, 42, 43, 44, 45
portraits 9, *11, 27, 37*
priests 8, 12, 13, *19*, 25
Ptah, god 29
pyramids 14, 15, 16-19, 21, 23, 30, 31, 45
queens 19, 43, 45
Ramesses II, pharaoh *8-9*, 34, 44
Ramesses IV, pharaoh 20
Re, god 18
religion 18, 19, 28, 29
rituals 13
sacrifices 40
sarcophaguses *10, 11, 20*, 27, 29

scanning machines 34
scarab beetles 23, 25
scientists 34, 35, 36, 42
servants *13*
shrines 25, 43
slaves 17
South America 38, 39, 41
spells 7, 8
Sphinx *21*, 23
star constellations 18, 19
statues *14, 19, 21*, 25, 26, *43*
steam engines 22
step pyramids *14*
teeth 35
temples 19, 28
thrones 7, *25*
Tollund Man 40
"tomb 55" 43
tomb robbers 15, 20-21, 24, 26
tombs 4, 6, 12, 16-19, 21
   mastaba 14, 19
   rock-cut *15, 20*, 21, 24-27, 42, 43, 44, 45
tools *17*
Tiy, Queen 43
Tutankhamun, pharaoh 23, 24-27, 30, 31, 42
Tuthmosis I, pharaoh 15
Underworld 6-7
Valley of the Golden Mummies 44
Valley of the Kings 15, 20, 24, 25, 43, 44
Washington Monument 23
workmen 16, 17
writing 33
X-rays 34
Zoser, pharaoh 14

Acknowledgements......................

Every effort has been made to trace the copyright holders of the material in this book. If any rights have been omitted, the publishers offer to rectify this in any subsequent editions following notification. The publishers are grateful to the following organizations and individuals for their permission to reproduce material (t=top, m=middle, b=bottom, l=left, r=right):

Cover © Getty Images/Derek P. Redfearn; **p1** © Pictor International; **p2** © Sandro Vannini/ CORBIS; **p3** ©Copyright The British Museum; **p4bl** ©Copyright The British Museum; **p4-5b** © Getty Images/Stephen Studd; **p5r** © Gianni Dagli Orti/CORBIS; **p6l** © Roger Wood/CORBIS; **p7** ©Copyright The British Museum; **p8tl** ©Copyright The British Museum; **p8-9b** © Kenneth Garrett/National Geographic Image Collection; **p9** ©Copyright The British Museum; **p10** ©Copyright The British Museum; **p11l, r** ©Copyright The British Museum; **p12bl** ©Copyright The British Museum; **p13** (l) © Gianni Dagli Orti/CORBIS, (r) ©Copyright The British Museum; **p14** (l) © Royalty-Free/CORBIS, (r) © Archivo Iconografico, S.A./CORBIS; **p15** © Roger Wood/CORBIS; **p16** © Andrew Bayuk; **p18-19b** © Getty Images/David Sutherland; **p19r** ©Copyright The British Museum; **p20** © Gianni Dagli Orti/CORBIS; **p21** (tr) ©Copyright The British Museum, (b) © Getty Images/PhotoLink; **p22** (l) © University College Museum, London, UK/Bridgeman Art Library, (r) © Bettmann/CORBIS; **p23** (t) © Getty Images/Hisham F. Ibrahim, (b) © ART on FILE/CORBIS; **p24** © Roger Wood/CORBIS; **p25** (tl) © Hulton-Deutsch Collection/CORBIS, (b) © AAA Collection Ltd.; **p26** (tr) © Griffith Institute, Oxford, (bl) © Robert Partridge: The Ancient Egypt Picture Library; **p27** (l) © Camera Press, (r) © TRIP/J Pilkington; **p28** (bl, br) ©Copyright The British Museum, (tr) © Gian Berto Vanni/CORBIS; **p28-29t** © Sandro Vannini/CORBIS; **p29r** ©Copyright The British Museum; **p30** (l) © Stapleton Collection/CORBIS, (r) © Robert Partridge: The Ancient Egypt Picture Library; **p31** (l) © CinemaPhoto/Corbis, (r) © Hammer/Kobal Collection; **p32** © Science Museum/Science and Society Picture Library; **p33** © Reuters; **p34** (l) ©Copyright The British Museum, (r) © Trustees of the National Museums of Scotland ; **p35** (t) © Peter Menzel/Science Photo Library, (br) © The Manchester Museum; **p36** (r) © Petrie Museum of Egyptian Archaeology, UCL.28614B; **p37** (tr) © Department of Archaeology, Bristol Museums and Art Gallery, (bl) ©Copyright The British Museum, (br) © University of Manchester (Fatima Head kept at the British Museum); **p38** © Chris Sharp/South American Pictures; **p39** © Robert Harding Picture Library/Alamy; **p40** © Chris Lisle/CORBIS; **p40-41b** © Viennareport/Camera Press; **p41t** ©Copyright The British Museum; **p42** (bl) © The Manchester Museum, (tr) © Getty Images/General Photographic Agency; **p43** (r) © Archivo Iconografico/CORBIS; **p44** © Sandro Vannini/CORBIS **p44-45t** © Ron Watts/CORBIS; **p45** (br) © Mediatheque EDF/Silicon Worlds.

Photographic manipulation by John Russell.